THE
Paleo
Bread
COOKBOOK

The JOY*ful* Table

Gluten & grain free breads, wraps,
crackers and more …

S U S A N   J O Y

CONTENTS

DEDICATION

To those who are missing their bread and crackers, while choosing to be healthier and nourishing their bodies and avoiding foods that may cause you harm.

Also, to my precious grandchildren: Emily, Harrison, Ruby, Jasper and Nathanael, who love taste testing my recipes and confirming they are kid friendly. Love you all to the moon and back!

A LITTLE ABOUT THE AUTHOR

Susan puts family first in everything. She has been married to Bryan for 44 wonderful years and has 3 adult sons, 3 amazing daughters-in-law and 5 precious grandchildren and she's hoping there will be more. Susan lives in Perth, Western Australia and is involved in her local church, teaching Sunday School to children aged from 5 to 8 years.

Susan suffered with chronic fatty liver disease and Hashimoto's thyroid disease for many years and found that changing to a Paleo lifestyle she was able to reverse her fatty liver disease and reduced the flare-ups from her autoimmune thyroid disease. Susan has also found that by removing refined sugars from her diet it substantially reduced her arthritic pain.

Her passion is to create delicious healthy recipes that the whole family will enjoy. Susan has written and published The JOYful Table cookbook - 'Paleo inspired recipes for good health and well-being', plus ebooks - A JOYful Christmas Table and The JOYful Table — 5 week meal plan. She runs a website filled with many wonderful recipes that the whole family will enjoy. Susan is a regular guest on 98.5fm radio (a local Perth radio station) and speaks at women's seminars on the benefits of healthy eating.

PHOTOGRAPHY BY
SUSAN JOY

INTRODUCTION

My desire to write this cookbook came from wanting to give a helping hand to those wishing to lead a healthy lifestyle but have struggled to give up their bread. I want to give you and your family better choices and still feel like you can have your bread and eat it too, whilst nourishing and nurturing your families wellbeing. I've also created several nut-free recipes for those with nut allergies and for adding to school lunchboxes.

I am so delighted that you have decided to bake your own bread, wraps, crackers and more…., and to leave behind all the additives and preservatives that come with most store-bought bread products. I commend you for choosing to eat grain and gluten free, avoiding phytic acid and lectins, plus the inflammation that comes with consuming them daily.

What we eat does matter and a diet of processed foods based on grains, refined sugars, preservatives and additives like colours and flavours, doesn't equate to good health.

In this book you will find recipes that you may have missed for quite some time and may have thought you wouldn't be able to eat them again. Well you will be pleasantly surprised with the choices you will find, like crumpets, olive ciabatta rolls, sourdough baguettes, crackers, tortillas, donuts, raisin bread, breadsticks, naan bread and so much more.

Happy and Joyful cooking!

Love Sue

One of the hardest foods I find people struggle to give up when starting a healthier way of eating is bread. You may have already chosen to cut gluten from your diet; as the impact of gluten in the body is more commonly understood these days. However, you may be struggling to move to the next step, which is cutting out all grains. This can be overwhelming as we rely heavily on bread for a quick and easy meal and I can hear you say, but what can I eat in place of bread? The answer is simple – you don't need to give up bread you just need a healthier substitute and that's why I've written this book to help you. Note though, that the texture will not be exactly like regular gluten and wheat products but in saying that, I have worked very hard to make my recipes as close as possible.

GOING GRAIN-FREE, WHAT DOES THIS MEAN?

A grain-free diet eliminates gluten containing grains as well as non-gluten grains. Grains include: wheat (couscous), spelt, barley, rye, corn (maize, millet), oats, rice, amaranth and sorghum. Grains react similarly in the body to sugar; they start to turn to sugar within several seconds of being in your mouth. Therefore, our body doesn't actually notice a big difference between sugars and grains at all. My body found this out the hard way but once I removed all grains and refined sugars from my diet I reversed my fatty liver disease.

BUT PEOPLE HAVE BEEN EATING GRAINS FOR THOUSANDS OF YEARS?

Modern day grains are nothing like ancient grains. Wheat and other grains have been genetically altered to provide processed food manufactures with the greatest yield at the lowest price. Consequently, they have been transformed into a food that is void of most nutrients causing our blood sugar to spike rapidly and contain addictive properties that cause/influence us to overeat. We also mill grains in the cheapest way possible (as opposed to traditionally stoneground by hand) and this also adds to the inflammation they cause.

DO GRAINS CAUSE ANY OTHER ISSUES?

Grains also cause problems to our gut because they contain compounds which are naturally designed to protect them. They have defense mechanisms called lectins and phytic acid (known as anti-nutrients). Lectins are like natural pesticides – toxic compounds meant to deter predators like bugs, birds or small animals that would like to have a meal. Phytic acid is found within the seeds of a plant and it actually protects the nutrients the seed needs to reproduce. Phytic acid binds to minerals in our body like zinc, calcium, iron and magnesium and affects how we absorb these nutrients. Lectins and phytic acid are also found in legumes – peanuts, lentils, kidney beans, navy beans, soy, chickpeas. So for example if you are someone who has a tendency to eat a piece of bread with every meal or each meal contains some sort of grain then as a result, overtime, our bodies can become depleted of these nutrients.

DON'T SOME NUTS CONTAIN PHYTIC ACID TOO?

It is true that there are certain nuts that contain phytic acid. Similar to grains, nuts also have natural defense mechanisms so they can survive and reproduce. However, on the bright side there is a lot of evidence to support the idea that if you soak, sprout or ferment foods that contain phytic acid then the phytic acid content is greatly reduced. The good news is that you can now even buy nuts which have been "activated" which means they have been soaked and dried again to enhance their vitamin and mineral absorption. If you cannot access "activated" then blanched (where the outer skin of the nut has been removed) is a great idea because most of the phytic acid lies in the skin. Overall nuts are still not as bad as grains as their lectin content is not as high, they don't contain gluten and generally don't irritate the gut/cause as much inflammation as grains. If you are concerned though remember to buy activated/blanched nuts and try not to consume them with each meal in order to maximize your nutrient levels.

SO HOW ARE GRAINS WITH GLUTEN EVEN WORSE?

Along with the anti-nutrients grains contain there is an extra problem with grains that also contain gluten. When flour is mixed with water gluten forms a sticky mix of proteins that give elastic properties to the dough (holds it together) and allows bread to rise when baked. The name gluten is actually derived from the word glue. When gluten reaches the digestive tract our immune system can react and mistake it for something foreign, like a bacteria. In certain people who are sensitive to gluten, it can cause the immune system to mount an attack against it. The immune system attacks the gluten proteins but it also attacks an enzyme in the cells of the digestive tract and in many people this causes an autoimmune response (our body starts to attack itself). This is how people develop a gluten sensitivity or celiac disease. Gluten is also know to be one of the most damaging foods to our gut. Overtime we can develop what is know as "leaky gut" which poses even more threat to our immune systems and can cause a whole host of health issues, (I now know this was how my autoimmune thyroid disease came about). Overall it is best to avoid gluten completely as it doesn't contain anything that our bodies need to thrive and remain healthy.

SO IF I BUY A PRODUCT THAT'S "GLUTEN-FREE" THEN IT'S HEALTHY, RIGHT?

Due to the number of people today that find they are reacting to gluten and grains or those choosing to eat healthier, manufactures have jumped on the bandwagon. They don't want to miss out on the market and are producing more gluten-free breads, wraps and crackers but are they healthy, do they have nutrients our bodies can use or recognize? Many contain rice and soy flour, they also use unhealthy oils like canola and vegetable (seed) oils, sugar and additives. The preservative 282 is found in many brands of breads, wraps and bakery products, it is added to extend the shelf life, make it soft and fluffy for longer and stop mold growing. (Calcium Propionate - 282 can be linked to migraines, irritable bowl, diarrhea, stomach pain, eczema, behavioral changes, sleep disturbance, bedwetting, foggy brain, nasal congestion and the list goes on and on). So please don't fall for the trap of assuming a gluten free product is a better substitute because in order for the product to taste as good then more additives and preservative need to be added.

SO WHAT DO I DO?

The best way to avoid all these unhealthy foods and additives that can deplete/degrade our health is to make your own bread, wraps and crackers. I've written this book just for those families that just can't give up their bread but want to still eat a healthy real food/Paleo diet. You will know exactly what is in the food you are eating. Now lets get started!

SUBSTITUTE INGREDIENTS USED FOR GRAIN FREE BREADS

ALMOND MEAL/FLOUR:

Almond meal is finely ground blanched almonds (you can also use ground whole almonds but it will produce a darker meal due to the skins). This nutritious nut has a slightly sweet flavour making it perfect for baked goods. Almond meal is an especially good source of vitamin E antioxidants and vitamin B. It is also high in fibre and contains iron, manganese, magnesium, potassium, calcium and other minerals. Nut meals are best stored in airtight containers in the fridge or freezer to prevent them going rancid.

ARROWROOT (TAPIOCA CAN BE USED IF STATED IN RECIPE):

Arrowroot is a large herb plant, the roots are cultivated for its starch properties. Combining arrowroot (or tapioca) with nut meals and grain-free flours help to bind all the ingredients, doing the job of gluten. The flour/starch also helps create a lighter texture. When arrowroot is harvested it is extracted in more traditional methods, without the use of high heat or harsh chemicals. Arrowroot is useful for those suffering with digestive issues or sensitivities, as it's gentle on the gut and has some healing benefits.

You can substitute tapioca for arrowroot (which may not be quite as gentle for people with chronic conditions). Tapioca flour is made from the dried roots of the cassava plant. When purchasing either flours, check they don't contain any preservatives (I've found brands in supermarkets can contain 202). They can also be labeled arrowroot and actually be tapioca as they are interchangeable in baking. Purchase pure arrowroot or tapioca from produce stores, health food stores or online.

CHIA SEEDS (BLACK AND WHITE):

These little seeds absorb approximately 9 times their weight in water and are excellent to bind and thicken baked goods. They can be grind down if you don't want to see little specks in your baking. (Chia seeds can also be used as an egg replacement in breads, muffins and cakes). There are many health benefits of chia seeds, they are a rich plant source of Omega 3 fats, dietary fibre and protein. Chia seeds are also packed with a variety of vitamins and minerals, antioxidants, amino acids and fatty acids.

CASHEWS NUTS:

Cashews nuts work well in baking once grind down to a flour. They have quite a delicate flavour and won't take away from other flavours in your baking. The oil in cashews are heart-protective fats that are similar to olive oil. Cashews are a rich source of dietary minerals, including copper, phosphorus, manganese, magnesium, selenium, iron and zinc.

COCONUT FLOUR (ORGANIC):

Coconut flour is made by drying and grinding coconut meat to a fine flour texture. Coconut flour is an excellent source of dietary fibre, protein and healthy fats. It's a good grain-free and nut-free alternative flour but does require a larger amount of liquid than normal when used for baked goods. I find it's best to combine the coconut flour with another grain-free meal or flour to prevent the texture being too dense in your baking. There are now quite a few brands of coconut flour available and they all seem to perform differently depending on how coarse the texture is, for best results choose a fine flour.

DESICCATED COCONUT (ORGANIC):

In the recipes calling for coconut I've used finely-shredded desiccated coconut. Make sure you are purchasing unsweetened and organic - many regular brands contain preservatives (sulphur dioxide).

GOLDEN FLAXSEED MEAL:

Golden flaxseed meal is finely ground golden linseed/whole flaxseed. It's just as nutritious and tasty as brown flaxseed meal but with a lighter colour for your baked goods. Flaxseed is full of Omega-3 essential fatty acids, the good fats for heart-health and is a key force against inflammation. It's very high in dietary fibre, containing both the insoluble and soluble types. Flaxseed is extremely low in carbohydrates (1 Tbsp = 0.1gms net carbs). It helps with binding ingredients in gluten-free baking and can also be used as an egg substitute when mixed with water. Keep refrigerated for freshness and to prevent the oils going rancid.

PSYLLIUM HUSKS AND POWDER:

Psyllium husks and powder are made up of insoluble and soluble dietary fibre (containing zero net carbs). Only a small quantity is needed to combine with other grain-free flours in recipes. Psyllium binds and holds moisture, it also helps baking rise and prevent crumbling. The husks expand when added to liquid and also work as an egg substitute. The powder is finely ground psyllium husks. You can purchase the husks and powder from the health food aisle in supermarkets and health food stores (you can make your own psyllium powder by using a blender or food processor and grind down to a very fine powder).

PUMPKIN SEEDS (PEPITAS):

Pumpkin seeds or pepitas are another nut-free option for grain free baking. They are an amazing health food and just a quarter cup of pumpkin seeds contains nearly half of the recommended daily amount of magnesium. Pumpkin seeds are small packages full of nutrition (plant based omega 3 fats, zinc and anti-inflammatory benefits).

SESAME SEEDS:

Sesame seeds can be used whole or ground down in baking. Sesame seeds have a rich, nutty flavour and have one of the highest oil contents of any seed. They provide high amounts of protein and dietary fibre. Sesame seeds are also rich in B vitamins and the dietary minerals, manganese, magnesium, calcium, iron and zinc. Keep refrigerated to prevent the oils going rancid.

SUNFLOWER SEEDS:

Sunflower seeds have a mild nutty flavour and are a great nut-free option. They are high in protein and contain high amounts of vitamin E. Vitamin E travels throughout the body neutralizing free radicals. Sunflower seeds are also a good source of magnesium.

OTHER INGREDIENTS AND FLAVOURINGS USED

APPLE CIDER VINEGAR:

Vinegar or an ingredient that is acidic is needed when using baking soda (bicarb) in baked goods. An acidic ingredient is required to activate it to rise and apple cider vinegar is a good choice for this due to its health benefits. Regular store-bought bread contains a flour-proofing additive, apple cider vinegar does the same thing (helping to preserve the bread). When purchasing, look for raw unfiltered apple cider vinegar 'with the mother' it has a cloudy appearance.

CACAO POWDER:

Raw cacao powder is not the same as cocoa powder, which has been heated and processed; it is raw and unsweetened. It has a stronger flavour and you would normally use less than cocoa powder. It is so good for you; high in dietary fibre, iron and is a good source of magnesium and antioxidants.

CINNAMON:

I am sure you will notice as you read my recipes that cinnamon appears quite frequently. The best cinnamon to use is Ceylon (Verum), commonly know as real or true cinnamon. It's not just eaten for its delicious sweet-warm flavour, it has huge health benefits in regulating blood sugar levels. Cinnamon also has antifungal properties and candida (yeast overgrowth) cannot live in a cinnamon environment. When added to foods it inhibits bacterial growth, making it a natural food preservative. These are just a few of the benefits.

COCONUT MILK AND CREAM:

I prefer to use canned coconut milk and cream as it's thicker and creamier to cook with than carton coconut milk (except for the crumpets). Read the labels, as even organic varieties can contain gums and thickeners. Ensure you purchase canned full-fat versions. I like to use Ayam Coconut Milk and Cream, as it's 100% coconut and comes in a BPA free can. (Always stir canned milk/cream well before using).

DRIED FRUIT:

Choose organic dried fruits that don't contain preservatives (sulphur) and are sun-dried and not coated in vegetable oil. I prefer Medjool dates but you can use any variety of date, if they are smaller, use 2 for each Medjool date and if they aren't moist, pop them in hot water for 15 minutes and drain.

FATS AND OILS:

Healthy fats are our brains best friend, so we need to eat the best quality. The nutritious fats I've used in my recipes are avocado oil, coconut oil, olive oil, macadamia oil, ghee and grass-fed butter. Highly processed oils derived from seeds and grains (like corn, soybean, canola, margarine and vegetable oils) must be avoided, as they are highly inflammatory to the body.

NUT AND SEED BUTTERS/SPREADS:

They help create a smoother texture to your baking. Make your own or purchase brands that are 100% nuts or seeds, avoid any with vegetable oils added. Store in the fridge after opening. Sunflower butter and tahini (hulled) can replace nut butters for nut-free baking.

NUTRITIONAL YEAST FLAKES:

Also know as Savoury Yeast Flakes. It's a fermented and deactivated yeast, which means it isn't going to grow. It has a creamy cheesy flavour and I've used it in a few recipes to create a cheese flavour. Vegans use it as a condiment and a cheese substitute, and to also add additional protein and vitamins to their diet (it's a complete protein). Nutritional yeast flakes are free from sugar, dairy, grains and gluten. Do not confuse it with yeast extract (MSG). Purchase from health food stores.

SALT:

Use organic sea salt, Celtic, pink Himalayan or Murry River salt in your baking, these salts come with all their 80 – 90 minerals intact. Avoid table salt at all cost, it's bleached and is stripped of its minerals and void of nutrients.

SWEETENERS:

I have used natural unrefined sweeteners in several recipes. I've attempted to reduce the amount of sweetness in the recipe to the lowest possible without compromising taste, feel free to adjust. Organic 100% maple syrup is a natural food sweetener (not flavoured maple syrup) and has a multitude of antioxidants and also contains manganese and zinc. When purchasing honey, choose a local unprocessed honey, it not only has wonderful health benefits but can help with allergies. Medjool Dates are moist, plump and full of fibre, they give a lovely caramel flavoured sweetness to recipes. Organic coconut sugar is produced from the sap of the coconut palm tree. I use it when a dry granular sweetener is required.

TIPS FOR SUCCESSFUL BAKING:

- When using my recipes I recommend having all your ingredients out and prepared before starting. Follow my recipe in its entirety. Once you have cooked a recipe and tasted my flavours and textures, then go ahead and experiment and adjust to your preferences.

- When measuring flours and other ingredients, I have used a level cup or spoon and also added grams where possible. Use the back of a knife to smooth over the top of the measuring cup or weigh on kitchen scales. When using coconut flour, ensure you measure exactly, as even the slightest difference may not get the results desired. (It's a very fibrous flour and absorbs a lot more liquid than other flours).

- Australian metric measurements have been used in the recipes. I have tried to make the measuring as uncomplicated as possible.

- If you use a different size baking tin, take note that baking times will vary.

- I have calculated cooking times using a fan-forced oven.

- I have used large eggs from a 700g carton.

- Wherever possible, I've used organic ingredients.

- My main equipment is a food processor or similar machine. Using a food processor when baking with nut meals, seeds and coconut flour will give you a more aerated and finer texture.

BREADS

Easy Low Carb Bread

This low carb loaf of bread is easily whipped up in not time. There's no need for a machine to blend the ingredients, just pop the dry ingredients into a bowl and add the wet and mix. It slices perfectly without crumbling due to the fine psyllium husk powder.

Makes: 1 loaf   **Prep time:** 10 mins   **Cooking time:** 60 mins

---

Ingredients

220g (2 cups) almond meal/flour (from blanched almonds)

40g (¼ cup) psyllium husk powder (not flakes)

3 Tbsp coconut flour

2 Tbsp gelatin – collagen hydrolysate* or protein powder

1 Tbsp baking powder (gluten free)

¾ tsp fine sea salt

5 large eggs, room temperature

2 tsp apple cider vinegar

60g (¼ cup) coconut oil, melted

125ml (½ cup) warm water

Sunflower seeds to sprinkle on top, optional

Directions

Preheat oven to 160c (fan-forced). Line a 21 x 10cm loaf tin with baking paper.

Add the almond meal, psyllium powder, coconut flour, gelatin, baking powder and salt to a large bowl. Lift the ingredients as you stir to aerate the fours.

Add the eggs and vinegar to a medium bowl and whisk. Pour the egg mixture and cooled coconut oil into the dry ingredients. Stir well, then pour in the warm water and mix to combine well.

Spoon the batter into the prepared tin and press down evenly with the back of the spoon. Dampen your hands and smooth the top surface and sprinkle with sunflower seeds, if using.

Bake for 60 – 65 minutes and a skewer inserted comes out clean and the top has a crisp hard crust. Cool in the tin for 15 minutes, then transfer to a wire rack to finish cooling.

Serve thinly sliced for sandwiches or toast. Store for up to 7 days, suitable to freeze for up to 3 months.

* Collagen hydrolysate peptide is gelatin that dissolves in liquid and this kind doesn't gel. It's 90% protein and helps with joint care, bones, skin and cartilage. I purchase the Great Lakes brand (green carton).

Artisan Bread

Artisan means hand crafted or free form bread, it's a more rustic looking bread. My Paleo Artisan bread has a crust that's thick and crusty, and tastes awesome toasted. You can also add other ingredients such as, sun-dried tomatoes, olives, garlic or herbs. It can be used in place of a ciabatta loaf but the texture doesn't have holes and lots of air like the original wheat/gluten loaf but is perfect to eat with cold meats, olives and picked vegetables.

Makes: 1 loaf   **Prep time:** 15 mins   **Cooking time:** 45 mins

Ingredients

220g (2 cups) almond meal/flour (from blanched almonds)

95g (¾ cup) arrowroot flour or tapioca

3 Tbsp psyllium husk powder (not flakes)

1 Tbsp coconut flour

1 Tbsp baking powder (gluten free)

¾ tsp baking soda (bicarb)

¾ tsp fine sea salt

150ml canned coconut milk

1 Tbsp apple cider vinegar

1 Tbsp 100% maple syrup

1 large egg

1 Tbsp olive oil, plus extra to spread over the dough

Directions

Preheat oven to 180c (fan-forced) and line a baking tray with baking paper.

Add the almond meal, arrowroot, psyllium powder, coconut flour, baking powder, baking soda and salt to a large bowl and stir well to mix and remove any lumps.

Warm the coconut milk, vinegar and maple syrup together and set aside (warm not hot).

Whisk the egg and oil together in a jug, then slowly drizzle in the warm coconut milk mixture while you whisk.

Pour the wet mixture into the dry ingredients and mix well to combine. Add a little olive oil to your hands and rub them together, then continue mixing with your hands until the dough has come together into a smooth ball of dough.

Place the dough on the prepared tray and shape into a 24cm smooth log with rounded ends. Use a sharp knife to cut 4 angled slices, 1cm deep across the top, this will reduce the cracking as the bread rises. Drizzle olive oil on the top and use your hands to evenly spread it over the top and sides.

Bake for 45 - 50 minutes, turn once while baking for an even colour. Allow to cool on the tray.

Serve while crusty with cold meats, olives and pickles (if the crust softens the next day, pop it back into the oven to crispen up). This bread is also delicious toasted and can be sliced and frozen.

Seed and Nut Bread

A delicious, nourishing bread that's full of protein and fibre from the seeds and nuts. It's low in carbs, packed with flavour and slices well without crumbling. When toasted it brings out the delicious walnut flavour.

Makes: 1 loaf   Prep time: 15 mins   Cooking time: 55 mins

Ingredients

4 large eggs

125ml (½ cup) coconut cream (a thick brand like Ayam)

1 Tbsp 100% maple syrup

2 tsp apple cider vinegar

140g (1¼ cups) almond meal/flour (from blanched almonds)

35g (⅓ cup) coconut flour

2 Tbsp golden flaxseed meal

1 Tbsp chia seeds

2 tsp baking powder (gluten free)

1 tsp mustard powder

1 tsp fine sea salt

½ cup walnuts

50g (⅓ cup) sunflower seeds

50g (⅓ cup) pumpkin seeds (pepitas)

1 Tbsp whole linseeds

Extra seeds for sprinkling on top

Directions

Preheat oven to 165c (fan-forced). Line a 21 x 10cm loaf tin with baking paper.

Add the eggs, coconut cream, maple syrup and apple cider vinegar to a food processor. Process for 5 – 6 seconds to blend the wet ingredients together.

Add the almond meal, coconut flour, golden flaxseed, chia seeds, baking powder, mustard powder and salt. Process for 10 seconds to produce a batter and then scrape down sides of the bowl.

Add the walnuts, sunflower seeds, pumpkin seeds and linseed to the batter. Process for approximately 3 seconds to distribute through the batter but not chop into pieces (you want them visible in the bread).

Spoon into the prepared tin and use damp fingers to press the batter into the corners and smooth the top surface.

Sprinkle a mix of sunflower, pumpkin seeds and whole linseed over the top and gently press to help them stick to the batter.

Bake for 55 minutes or until crisp on top and cooked through. Allow to cool in the tin for 15 minutes before removing then finish cooling on a wire rack.

Store in an airtight container in the fridge for up to 7 days or freeze sliced for up to 3 months.

Sesame Sandwich Loaf (nut-free)

A delicious nut-free, light and fluffy loaf that rises beautifully and slices like traditional bread. It's a perfect loaf for making sandwiches.

Serves: 1 loaf Prep time: 15 mins Cooking time: 1 hour

Ingredients

128g (1 cup) arrowroot or tapioca flour

120g (1 cup) golden flaxseed meal

80g (½ cup) sesame seeds

2 Tbsp psyllium husk powder (not flakes)

2 tsp coconut sugar, optional

1½ tsp mustard powder

2 tsp baking powder (gluten free)

1 tsp baking soda (bicarb)

¾ tsp sea salt

4 large eggs

3 Tbsp avocado oil (for nut-free) or macadamia oil

2 tsp apple cider vinegar

180ml (¾ cup) filtered water

White and black sesame seeds to sprinkle on top, optional

Directions

Preheat oven to 180c (fan-forced). Line a 21 x 10cm loaf tin with baking paper, leave a small overhang of paper to help when removing bread.

Add the arrowroot flour, golden flaxseed, sesame seeds, psyllium powder, coconut sugar, mustard powder, baking powder, soda and salt to a food processor. Process for 20 seconds to break down the sesame seeds to create a fine texture.

Have all the wet ingredients measured and ready for the next step.

Add the eggs, oil, vinegar and water. Process to mix well without delay, approximately 10 – 12 seconds to produce a smooth mixture (the moisture absorbs quickly).

Transfer the mixture into the prepared tin, press down using wet fingers to compact the mixture and level the top. Sprinkle with a mix of white and black sesame seeds, press down lightly to help them stick to the dough.

Bake for approximately 1 hour. The top will be crunchy after 45 minutes but continue cooking longer so the centre cooks through. Allow the bread to cool in the tin for 10 minutes, then lift out by the paper and finish cooling on a wire rack.

Once completely cooled, slice thinly and store in an airtight container or freeze. Keeps for up to 10 days stored in the fridge and 3 months in the freezer.

Note: Due to flaxseed and psyllium powder absorbing liquid quite fast, you may need to work quickly after liquid is added. *Psyllium husk powder can be purchased or make it yourself by grinding to a fine powder using a blender.

Delicious
White Paleo Bread

A grain-free white loaf of bread which will suit those that miss regular white sliced bread. Suitable for children that don't like dense seed and nut paleo breads, it's perfect for sandwiches and for toasting.

Makes: 1 loaf   Prep time: 15 mins   Cooking time: 45 mins

Ingredients   ½ cup Whey

165g (~~1½ cups~~) *1 cup* almond meal/flour (from blanched almonds)

128g (1 cup) arrowroot flour or tapioca

26g (¼ cup) coconut flour

3 Tbsp golden flaxseed meal

½ tsp baking soda (bicarb)

2 tsp baking powder (gluten free)

¾ tsp sea salt

4 large whole eggs

2 large egg whites

125ml (½ cup) almond or cashew milk

1 Tbsp 100% maple syrup

2 tsp apple cider vinegar

Directions

Preheat oven to 170c (fan-forced). Line a 21 x 10cm loaf tin with baking paper.

Add the almond meal, arrowroot, coconut flour, flaxseed, baking soda, baking powder and salt to a food processor. Process for 18 - 20 seconds to create a fine texture to the flours.

Add the whole eggs, egg whites, maple syrup, almond milk and vinegar. Process for 20 seconds to combine and produce a cake-like smooth batter.

Spoon into the prepared tin and use a spatula to smooth the top.

Bake for 45 - 50 minutes until the top is golden and the bread is coming away from the sides of the pan.

Store in an airtight container. Suitable to freeze, slice before freezing.

Note: If you are using regular ground flaxseed, the bread will be darker in colour.

Paleo Rye Bread

This is a delicious rye-style bread that contains no actual rye. It's perfect for those wanting a healthier, nutrient dense bread option with a full flavour. Serve spread with mustard and topped with corned silverside and sauerkraut for lunch or toasted with eggs and avocado for breakfast.

Makes: 1 loaf   **Prep time:** 15 mins   **Cooking time:** 60 mins

Ingredients

220g (2 cups) almond meal (from blanched almonds)

75g (⅔ cups) golden flaxseed meal

3 Tbsp psyllium husk powder

2 Tbsp raw cacao powder, sifted

1½ Tbsp maca powder, sifted (gives a malt flavour)

3 tsp baking powder (gluten free), sifted

1 tsp baking soda (bicarb), sifted

1½ tsp caraway seeds

1 tsp fine sea salt

3 large eggs

120g (½ cup) coconut cream or natural coconut yoghurt

80ml (⅓ cup) olive oil or macadamia

1 Tbsp apple cider vinegar

125ml (½ cup) warm water

1 Tbsp molasses (unsulphed)

Directions

Preheat oven to 170c (fan-forced). Line a 21 × 10cm loaf tin with baking paper.

Add the almond meal, flaxseed meal and psyllium powder to a large bowl, then sift in the cacao, maca, baking powder, baking soda and salt. Add in the caraway seeds (you can crush them or add whole) and stir all the dry ingredients to combine well.

Whisk the eggs in a medium bowl, then add in the coconut cream/yoghurt, oil and vinegar, and whisk well into the eggs.

Add the warm water and molasses to a small jug and stir.

Pour the egg mixture into the bowl of dry ingredients and mix well, then add in the warm water mixture. Stir well to bring all the ingredients together to form a ball. Place into the prepared tin and use your fingers to push the dough out evenly and smooth the top. For a glossy finish, brush some egg white over the top.

Bake for 60 minutes or until crisp on top and coming away from the sides of the tin. Allow to cool in the tin for 15 minutes, then transfer to a wire rack to finish cooling.

Cut into thin slices once completely cooled. Store in an airtight container in the fridge for up to 7 days. This bread freezes well and is delicious toasted.

Crumpets (egg-free)

Making crumpets is surprisingly simple and I wouldn't have thought of making them if I hadn't had so many requests. To create the crumpet texture dried yeast is required and a little time for proving (choose a yeast without additives, Saccharomyces cerevisiae is the type for baking bread). You can't beat homemade crumpets, they taste so much better than store-bought ones.

Makes: 6   **Prep time:** 15 mins (plus proving)   **Cooking time:** 15 mins

Ingredients

200ml organic coconut milk, from a carton

1 tsp unprocessed honey

½ Tbsp (6g) dried yeast

85g (¾ cup) almond meal/flour (from blanched almonds)

95g (¾ cup) arrowroot flour/starch (not tapioca for this recipe)

½ tsp fine sea salt

¼ tsp baking soda (bicarb)

Olive oil for greasing

Directions

Warm the coconut milk and honey together, and then pour into a small jug. Sprinkle in the yeast and whisk with a fork to dissolve. Leave the jug in a warm place for approximately 15 minutes or until the mixture becomes frothy.

Add the almond meal, arrowroot, salt and baking soda to a large bowl. Stir to combine the ingredients and make a well in the centre. Pour in the yeast mixture and quickly whisk from the centre to outwards for 2 – 3 minutes to create a smooth consistency with no lumps and to add extra air. It will become a little thicker after proving.

Cover the bowl with a tea towel and set aside in a warm place for 45 minutes or until the batter has a cream top, slightly risen and has some little bubbles around the edges.

Heat a large frying pan on medium-low heat. Grease 3 x 9cm crumpet rings (or large egg rings) well with olive oil and smear a little oil over the pan. Arrange the rings in the frying pan and once hot, pour in ¼ cup of the batter into each ring (you can also use 10cm mini spring form cake tins and remove the bases and use the sides as a ring).

Cook for 5 minutes or until the bubbles on top have burst and left holes, also the colour will change to cream and not look as wet. Use tongs to carefully lift off the rings, then turn the crumpets over using a spatula. Cook the second side for 40–60 seconds to give a light colouring to the tops. The bottoms will be dark brown. (If you find the crumpet sticks when lifting off the ring, run a knife carefully around the inside, it will come off easier if you remove the ring before the crumpet bottom is too crisp).

Place the cooked crumpets on a wire rack in a single layer and re-grease the rings before cooking the remaining batter (take care as rings will be hot).

Serve the crumpets warm and if you are making them in advance, just pop in a toaster and toast lightly just before serving.

For a savoury snack it's fun to add pizza toppings and then pop in the oven.

Turkish Bread

My version of Turkish bread isn't quite as fluffy as the traditional wheat version but it's so tasty and is a perfect replacement for those that are missing the gluten variety. It has a crispy top and a delicious flavour from the caraway and sesame seeds.

Serves: 6 - 8   **Prep time:** 15 mins   **Cooking time:** 30 mins

Ingredients

250g (2¼ cups) almond meal/flour (from blanched almonds)

95g (¾ cup) arrowroot flour or tapioca

1 Tbsp coconut flour

1 Tbsp baking powder (gluten free)

1 tsp caraway seeds

¾ tsp fine sea salt

125ml (½ cup) canned coconut milk (a thick brand like Ayam)

125ml filtered water

1 large egg

1 Tbsp olive oil, plus extra for the top

White and black sesame seeds to sprinkle on top

Directions

Preheat oven to 180c (fan-forced). Line a large baking tray with baking paper.

Add the almond meal, arrowroot, coconut flour, baking powder, caraway seeds and salt to a large bowl. Stir to mix and remove any lumps.

Add the coconut milk and water, and then stir well to remove any clumps in the mixture.

Whisk the egg and olive oil together in a small bowl and pour into the mixture. Mix well to create a smooth thick batter (it's quite a sticky mixture).

Spoon the mixture onto the prepared tray and use the back of a spoon that's dampened with water to spread out to approximately 30 x 18cm with rounded corners.

To give a Turkish bread look, dip your finger into a little olive oil and poke dimples into the dough (the oil will prevent the dough sticking to your finger). Sprinkle white and black sesame seeds over the top.

Place into the oven and bake for 15 minutes then remove and drizzle olive oil evenly over the top, this will help add a little colour and crispness to the top. Return to the oven and bake for a further 15 minutes. Allow to cool on the tray.

Serve with olive oil and balsamic vinegar, your favourite dip or pickled vegetables. It's best eaten on the day but will keep for up to 3 days in an airtight container. Suitable to freeze.

Garlic Bread

Delicious and crispy garlic bread made from low-carb ingredients. Bake to eat with your favourite Italian meal or add to a platter of finger foods at your next party.

Makes: 16 pieces   **Prep time:** 20 mins   **Cooking time:** 40 mins

Ingredients

110g (1 cup) almond meal/flour (from blanched almonds)

40g (¼ cup) psyllium husk powder (not flakes)

2 Tbsp coconut flour

2 tsp baking powder (gluten free)

¾ tsp fine sea salt

2 large eggs

1 Tbsp olive oil

1 Tbsp apple cider vinegar

180ml warm filtered water

GARLIC BUTTER SPREAD

60g (¼ cup) ghee or grass-fed butter, soft

1 tsp garlic, minced

Pinch fine sea salt

1 Tbsp finely chopped parsley

Directions

Preheat oven to 170c (fan-forced). Line a baking tray with baking paper.

Add the almond meal, psyllium powder, coconut flour, baking powder and salt to a large bowl. Stir well to combine and remove any lumps.

Add the eggs, olive oil and apple cider vinegar to a small bowl and whisk. Pour into the bowl of dry ingredients and stir well. Add the warm water and mix to create a smooth dough.

Divide the dough into 8 equal portions and roll each between your palms to make log shapes, approximately 10cm in length. Place them on the prepared tray and press to slightly flatten.

Bake for 40 – 45 minutes or until lightly brown and the bottoms are crisp. Allow the buns to cool.

Combine the garlic butter spread ingredients in a small bowl and set aside.

Heat the oven to 180c (fan-forced). Use a serrated knife to halve the buns lengthways. Spread the soft side of the buns generously with the garlic spread and place them back onto the tray. Bake for 15 – 20 minutes depending on how crisp you prefer your garlic bread.

Serve warm with your meal or as an appetizer.

Sourdough Baguettes

By making a cashew sourdough culture you can create a tasty baguette. These paleo baguettes have crunchy crusts and are perfect to pull apart or slice lengthways and eat with sandwich fillings. You can ferment the cashews in a warm place or in a yoghurt maker. It's also fine to make this bread without fermenting but you lose flavour.

Makes: 2   **Prep time:** 15 mins (plus fermenting time)   **Cooking time:** 25 mins

Ingredients

250g raw cashews

125ml (½ cup) filtered water

2 good quality probiotic capsules (Acidophilus, non-dairy brand)

160g (1¼ cups) arrowroot flour or tapioca

38g (⅓ cup) golden flaxseed meal

¾ tsp baking soda (bicarb)

¾ tsp sea salt

2 tsp apple cider vinegar

1 large egg

Directions

To create the sourdough culture: Add the cashews to a food processor or blender and process to make a nut meal texture. Add the water and blend to create a smooth paste with no grainy bits, scrape down sides. Break open the probiotic capsules and add the contents. Blend for a few seconds to mix the probiotics through the cashew paste. Transfer to a ceramic or glass bowl and cover (I wrap my bowl in a beeswax wrap). Set aside in a warm place to ferment for approx. 24 hours. In hot weather time can be reduced and cold weather it may need to be lengthened (check for a slight sour taste).

To make the bread: Preheat oven to 170c (fan-forced) and line a large baking tray.

Add the cashew culture to a food processor with the remaining ingredients and process for 25 seconds to create a smooth batter. Remove the blade and scrape down the sides. Allow to sit for 5 minutes to thicken.

Divide the batter into 2 portions and spoon each onto the lined tray. Use damp hands to shape the portions into 30cm long logs (the batter will be quite sticky).

Add a little arrowroot flour to your hands and lightly dust over the top of each log. Use a knife dusted in arrowroot to make 5 angled slices in the top of each baguette, 0.5cms deep (this will help prevent the crust splitting too much as they rise).

Bake for 25 - 30 minutes or until a skewer inserted comes out clean. The outside will be lovely and crunchy.

Enjoy these crunchy baguettes pulled apart or cut in half and sliced opened to create a sandwich. Best eaten on the same day.

NOTE: If you are using regular ground flaxseed the bread colour will be a little darker but it won't affect the flavour.

Damper

Damper is a traditional Australian soda bread that was baked in the coals of a campfire by swagmen, drovers and stockmen. It's quite a heavy bread but it was very filling for the workers. This version is made with almond meal which also makes it a dense bread. It's the perfect bread for dipping into the gravy of stews and casseroles.

Makes: 8 portions   **Prep time:** 15 mins   **Cooking time:** 30 mins

Ingredients

330g (3 cups) almond meal/flour (from blanched almonds)

95g (¾ cup) arrowroot flour or tapioca

2 tsp coconut sugar

1½ tsp baking soda (bicarb)

1½ tsp baking powder (gluten free)

½ tsp dried caraway seeds

½ tsp fine sea salt

3 large eggs

1 Tbsp apple cider vinegar

Black sesame seeds to sprinkle on top

Directions

Preheat oven to 170c (fan-forced). Line a baking tray with baking paper.

Add the almond meal, arrowroot, coconut sugar, baking soda, baking powder, caraway seeds and salt to a large bowl. Mix to combine and remove any lumps.

Add the eggs and apple cider vinegar to a small bowl and whisk together. Pour into the bowl of dry ingredients and mix with a large spoon then finish mixing with your hands to create a moist dough.

Dust your hands with arrowroot and transfer the dough to the prepared tray and shape it into a circle that's approximately, 15cm in diameter and 3cm high. Lightly dust the top and sides with a little arrowroot four, then sprinkle the top with black sesame seeds and press them down lightly to help them stick (if you have too much arrowroot the seeds will have trouble sticking).

Dust a large knife with arrowroot and score the top of the bread. Cut firstly into quarters and then into eighths, make the cuts 1.5cm deep.

Bake for 30 minutes or until lightly golden and a hard crust has formed. Allow to sit for 10 minutes before serving.

Serve with soups, stews or with eggs for breakfast spread with grass-fed butter or ghee.

English Muffins

So easy, just pop everything into a blender and whiz. After baking, slice the muffins and fry them in ghee to give the English muffin look, which also adds to their delicious flavour.

Serves: 4   **Prep time:** 10 mins   **Cooking time:** 25 mins

---

Ingredients

75g (⅔ cup) almond meal/flour (from blanched almonds)

2½ Tbsp golden flaxseed meal

2 tsp baking powder (gluten free)

½ tsp fine sea salt

3 large eggs

125ml (½ cup) canned coconut milk (a thick brand like Ayam)

1 Tbsp macadamia oil, plus extra to grease ramekins

Ghee for frying the halved muffins

Directions

Preheat oven to 180c (fan-forced). Grease four, 9cm ramekins generously with the extra macadamia oil.

Add all the above ingredients, except for the ghee, to a blender. Start on variable speed to mix the ingredients and increase to high for 3 – 4 seconds.

Pour the batter evenly between the prepared ramekins. Place them on a baking tray and bake for 25 minutes or until the muffins are lightly golden and just starting to come away from the sides.

Allow to cool in the ramekins for 10 – 15 minutes. Use a knife to run around the sides to loosen the muffins and remove (if you find the bottoms stick a little, you can place a circle of baking paper on the bases).

Use a serrated knife to slice the muffins in half. Heat a frying pan on medium heat and add some ghee. Place the cut muffins in the pan and use a spatula to press down on them to lightly brown. Flip to cook second side, this will make them look like an English muffin.

Serve topped with a fried egg for breakfast or children may like them spread with almond or sunflower butter, or homemade jam topped with coconut yoghurt.

To freeze, place paper between the cooled fried slices and seal in an airtight container (once thawed you can pop them into a toaster to reheat).

Light and Fluffy Bread Rounds (nut-free)

A low-carb, light textured alternative for sliced bread. It can be used for sandwiches, for spreads like pate or for dipping into gravies. I also found they work really well folded; pop in a filling, then fold the round in half and insert a tooth pick to hold it closed and serve as an appetizer.

Makes: 8   **Prep time:** 15 mins   **Cooking time:** 20 mins

Ingredients

3 large eggs, separated (at room temperature)

80g (⅓ cup) natural coconut yoghurt

2 Tbsp golden flaxseed meal

1 tsp baking powder (gluten free)

⅓ tsp fine sea salt

2 Tbsp finely sliced chives or coriander, optional

Directions

Preheat oven to 150c (fan-forced). Line 2 baking trays with baking paper.

Separate the eggs and place the whites and salt into a medium glass or stainless steal bowl. Beat the egg whites until you reach firm peaks. Set aside.

Place the egg yolks, coconut yoghurt, flaxseed and baking powder into a large bowl and mix well using a fork.

Gently fold the egg whites through the yolk mixture trying to keep the air in the mixture.

Scoop out 8 equal portions of mixture onto the prepare trays, approximately a ¼ cup for each. Use the back of a spoon to help spread out the mixture to form 10cm rounds.

Bake for 20 – 25 minutes until golden in colour (the bottom tray may need a few extra minutes). Cool the bread rounds on the trays, once cooled remove by peeling them off the paper or slide a spatula under to remove.

Store in an airtight container in the fridge for up to 3 days.

Cob Loaf

This large loaf of bread is baked in a cake tin to create the round shape of a cob loaf. It's high in omega 3 fatty acids and protein from the chia seeds, the chia also helps hold this lovely textured loaf together and prevents crumbling. As the bread is quite light, it's excellent as a sandwich bread. The top can be sliced off and some of the centre removed to fill with your favourite dip. It can also be cooked in an extra large bread tin if you prefer a regular bread shape.

Makes: 1 large loaf   **Prep time:** 15 mins   **Cooking time:** 60 mins

Ingredients

45g (¼ cup) chia seeds

125ml filtered water

6 large eggs

350g cashew butter/spread

160ml almond milk or milk of choice

1 Tbsp apple cider vinegar

52g (½ cup) coconut flour

32g (¼ cup) arrowroot flour or tapioca

2 tsp baking powder (gluten free)

1½ tsp baking soda (bi carb)

1 tsp fine sea salt

Directions

Preheat oven to 160c (fan-forced). Place a sheet of baking paper over the base of a 20cm spring form cake tin and clip the sides closed. Grease the sides of the tin generously with coconut oil.

Add the chia seeds and water to a small bowl and mix well. Set aside to soak for 10 minutes to form a gel.

Add the eggs, cashew butter, milk, vinegar and chia mixture to a food processor. Process for 15 seconds to combine well, then scrape down the sides of the bowl.

Add the coconut flour, arrowroot, baking powder, baking soda and salt. Process for 20 seconds, this mixture will resemble a cake batter texture.

Pour into the prepared cake tin and bake for 60 – 65 minutes until golden and firm to the touch and a skewer inserted comes out clean.

Cool in the tin for 20 minutes, then run a spatula or knife around the inside edge and remove the spring sides. Finish cooling the bread on a wire rack.

Store in the fridge for up to 10 days or freeze sliced for up to 3 months.

Raisin Bread (nut-free)

You don't have to miss out on raisin toast anymore. This loaf is lightly spiced and is sweetened with organic dried fruit and contains no nuts.

Serves: 1 loaf   **Prep time:** 20 mins   **Cooking time:** 1 hour

Ingredients

128g (1 cup) arrowroot or tapioca flour

120g (1 cup) golden flaxseed meal

80g (½ cup) sesame seeds

2 Tbsp psyllium husk powder (not flakes)

1½ Tbsp cinnamon

2 tsp allspice

2 tsp baking powder (gluten free)

1 tsp baking soda (bicarb)

¾ tsp sea salt

4 large eggs

2 Tbsp honey (unprocessed)

3 Tbsp avocado oil (for nut-free) or macadamia oil

2 tsp apple cider vinegar

2 tsp vanilla extract (organic)

180ml (¾ cup) filtered water

⅓ - ½ cup sultanas (organic)

4 – 5 Medjool dates, finely chopped

1 egg white, lightly whisked for glazing, optional

Directions

Preheat oven to 180c (fan-forced). Line a 21 x 10cm loaf tin with baking paper, leave a small overhang of paper to help when removing the bread.

Add the arrowroot, flaxseed, sesame seeds, psyllium powder, cinnamon, allspice, baking powder, soda and salt to a food processor. Process for 20 seconds to break down the sesame seeds to create a fine texture.

Have all the wet ingredients and dried fruit measured and ready for the next step (the moisture will be absorbed quickly when added).

Add the eggs, honey, oil, vinegar, vanilla and water. Process for approximately 10 – 12 seconds to mix well and produce a smooth mixture. Remove blade and stir through the dried fruit before the mixture thickens.

Scoop dough into the prepared tin, if the dough has firmed up, use wet fingers to compact and level the top.

Bake for 45 minutes, remove and brush the top with the egg white. Return to the oven and continue cooking for a further 15 minutes. Allow the bread to cool in the tin for 10 minutes, then lift out by the paper and allow too finish cooling on a wire rack.

Once completely cooled, store in an airtight container in the fridge for up to 10 days or slice and freeze.

BREAD ROLLS

Olive Ciabatta Rolls (nut & egg-free)

The one loaf of bread I really missed when I changed to eating Paleo all those years ago, was Italian Olive Ciabatta, it was our weekend treat. I've made my ciabatta bread into the size of dinner rolls. My hubby has Italian roots and he has given great reviews on this recipe. You won't find any nuts or eggs in this bread and if you don't like olives, just leave them out.

Makes: 12   **Prep time:** 15 mins   **Cooking time:** 40 mins

Ingredients

128g (1 cup) arrowroot flour or tapioca

26g (¼ cup) coconut flour, sifted

2 Tbsp psyllium husk powder (not flakes)

2 tsp baking powder (gluten free)

1 tsp fine sea salt

125ml (½ cup) canned coconut milk (a thick brand like Ayam)

2 Tbsp olive oil

1 Tbsp apple cider vinegar

160ml warm filtered water

½ cup pitted Kalamata olives, sliced

Directions

Preheat oven to 190c (fan-forced). Line a large baking tray with baking paper.

Add the arrowroot, coconut flour, psyllium powder, baking powder and salt to a large bowl. Stir to mix well then make a well in the middle.

Add the coconut milk, oil and vinegar into the middle and mix, then start incorporating into the dry ingredients making sure to break up any lumps in the mixture.

Add the warm water and olives and stir quickly to distribute the olives evenly before the mixture thickens. Add a little olive oil to your hands and rub palms together, this will prevent the mixture sticking, then mix using your hands and form a ball of dough.

Use your hands to scoop out 12 equal portions, roughly 2 heaped tablespoons for each bread roll. Use oiled hands to roll the mixture into balls and place evenly spaced over the prepared tray. Press gently down on each bread roll to slightly flatten, so they look like dinner rolls.

Bake for 40 minutes (yes that long) until cooked all the way through. Their bottoms should sound hollow when tapped (if you take them out too soon the rolls will sink in the middle).

Cool on the tray before serving (the middle can still be a bit soft until cooled). Best eaten crisp on the day but they can be put back into a hot oven to crispen up. They can also be frozen and once thawed added to a hot preheated oven for 10 minutes.

Bread Rolls

These bread rolls have a lovely soft and light texture and are so quick to make. They are perfect to use with hamburgers or you can make them into log shaped rolls to make subs.

Makes: 6   Prep time: 10 mins   Cooking time: 25 mins

Ingredients

165g (1½ cups) almond meal/flour (from blanched almonds)

35g (⅓ cup) coconut flour

2 Tbsp psyllium husk powder (not flakes)

2 tsp baking powder (gluten free)

1 tsp baking soda (bicarb)

½ tsp fine sea salt

2 large eggs

2 tsp 100% maple syrup

200g natural coconut yoghurt (or Greek)

Poppy seeds or sesame seeds to sprinkle on top (optional)

Directions

Preheat oven to 180c (fan-forced). Line a baking tray with baking paper.

Add the almond meal, coconut flour, psyllium powder, baking powder, baking soda, and salt to a food processor. Process for 10 seconds to mix well and create a finer texture.

Add the eggs, maple syrup and yoghurt (If your yoghurt is very firm or solid add 1 tablespoon of coconut milk or water). Process for approximately 20 seconds to combine all the ingredients well. Allow to sit for 3 – 4 minutes to allow absorption.

Scoop out 6 equal portions of mixture onto the lined tray. Use your hands to shape into round patty or log shaped rolls (if the mixture is too sticky, dampen your hands to shape but it does firm up). Optional, sprinkle the tops with seeds and press down lightly to help them stick.

Bake for 25 minutes until golden. Turn once while cooking for an even colour. Allow to completely cool before slicing.

Best eaten on the same day but can be stored in an airtight container for up to 3 days (if needed they can be freshened up by popping back into a preheated oven for 5 – 8 minutes). Suitable to freeze.

Muffin Bread Rolls (nut-free)

These quick and easy muffin style bread rolls are whipped up in minutes. Kids will love the soft and fluffy centres, and being nut-free they are perfect for lunch boxes. Delicious sliced with grass-fed butter or your favourite spread. I love these buns with soup and also fried in the pan with my eggs for breakfast. If you tolerate a little dairy, you might like to stir in ½ cup of grated aged cheese.

Makes: 10   **Prep time:** 10 mins   **Cooking time:** 40 mins

Ingredients

2 large eggs

180ml (¾ cup) canned coconut milk (use a thick brand like Ayam)

80ml (⅓ cup) filtered water

80ml (⅓ cup) mild flavoured olive oil

1 tsp 100% maple syrup (or sweetener of choice)

160g (1¼ cups) arrowroot flour (tastes better with arrowroot but tapioca can be used)

75g (⅔ cup) golden flaxseed meal

1 tsp dry mustard powder

¾ tsp fine sea salt

½ tsp baking soda (bicarb)

Directions

Preheat oven to 180c (fan-forced). Use a large silicone muffin tray or add paper liners to a muffin tin (they pop out really easily from the silicone tray).

Add all the ingredients to a food processor in the above order. Blend for 30 seconds. The mixture will thicken very quickly, so don't delay in getting the batter into the muffin tray.

Use 2 spoons to fill the muffin cups ¾ full. Scoop the batter out with one spoon and use the second to push the mixture off into the cups. If the batter gets overly thick, wet the back of a spoon to smooth the tops and help press and spread the batter evenly.

Bake for approximately 40 – 45 minutes or until the bread rolls are lightly golden on top and cooked through (if under cooked that can sink a little). Let them cool in the tray for 5 – 10 minutes and serve warm.

The bread rolls keep fresh for up to 3 days in an airtight container at room temperature. They freeze well and keep for up to 3 months frozen.

NOTE: If you use regular ground flaxseed the rolls will be a little darker in colour, but no difference in flavour. They can also be mixed by hand, first add the dry ingredients to a bowl, stir, then add the wet ingredients and mix well to make a smooth mixture.

Hamburger Buns (nut-free)

These nut-free discs of paleo bread have a lovely light, soft texture and they hold all your burger ingredients together. They also work well for sandwiches. They are actually one of my favourite breads, I love their soft texture and they taste a bit like a savoury pumpkin scone.

Makes: 4 sets (8 pieces)   **Prep time:** 10 mins   **Cooking time:** 20 mins

Ingredients

26g (¼ cup) coconut flour

3 Tbsp arrowroot flour or tapioca

2 Tbsp golden flaxseed meal

½ tsp baking soda (bicarb)

¼ tsp fine sea salt

Pinch ground pepper

180g of peeled pumpkin, cubed

1 tsp apple cider vinegar

2 large eggs

80ml (⅓ cup) filtered water

Directions

Preheat oven to 180c (fan-forced). Line 2 baking trays with baking paper.

Add the coconut four, arrowroot, flaxseed, baking soda, salt, pepper and uncooked chopped pumpkin to a food processor. Process for 40 seconds or until you have a moist fine mixture with no pumpkin pieces visible. Stop halfway and scrape down the sides and base of the bowl.

Add the vinegar, eggs and water, and process for approximately 45 - 50 seconds to create a smooth spreadable mixture.

Scoop out 8 equal portions of the mixture onto the prepared trays (approximately 2½ tablespoons per portion). Use the back of a spoon to spread the mixture out to form a 10cm diameter disc/round.

Bake for 20 minutes or until firm to the touch and lightly brown.

Store in an airtight container for up to 4 days. When freezing, separate with pieces of baking paper.

Hot Dog Buns

These buns are perfect to cradle your additive-free hot dog or sausage in. I created this recipe after receiving a message from a young mother. She wanted her daughter to be able to have a gluten/grain free bun to take to parties, she didn't want her to feel left out and wanted the bun to look similar to the other kids. I've used yeast in this recipe to help create a soft-centred bun (choose a yeast without additives, Saccharomyces cerevislae is the type for bread).

Makes: 4 or 6 kid size   **Prep time:** 20 mins   **Cooking time:** 35 mins

Ingredients

350ml warm filtered water (42c/107f - not too hot or yeast won't foam)

2 tsp (7g) dried yeast

1 Tbsp 100% maple syrup

150g (1⅓ cups) almond meal/flour (from blanched almonds)

128g (1 cup) arrowroot flour or tapioca

35g (⅓ cup) coconut flour

2 Tbsp psyllium husk powder (not flakes)

1 Tbsp golden flaxseed meal

1¼ tsp fine sea salt

Olive oil or melted ghee to brush over buns

Directions

Pour the warm water into a jug or bowl and whisk in the yeast. Add the maple syrup and stir (the yeast will feed on the maple syrup). Allow to sit for 15 minutes while foam forms on top.

Meanwhile, add the almond meal, arrowroot, coconut flour, psyllium powder, flaxseed and salt to a large bowl. Stir well and remove any lumps.

Pour the warm foaming mixture into the dry ingredients and mix well to combine. Let the dough sit for 2 minutes to allow the moisture to be absorbed, then knead the dough for 45 - 60 seconds. Cover the bowl with a tea towel and let sit in a warm spot out of a draught for 1 hour.

Preheat oven to 190c (fan-forced) 10 minutes before the proving has finished. Line a baking tray with baking paper.

Divide the risen dough into 4 equal portions (approx. 168g each) or 6 portions for kid size buns (approx. 112g each). Coat your palms with olive oil and shape the portions into round logs, then roll the logs between your palms to make the surface smooth, add extra oil to your palms as needed. Make the 4 portions 17cm long (the kid size 12 - 13cms).

Place the dough portions on the prepared tray and wipe olive oil or melted ghee over the tops and sides. Slice a 1cm deep cut down the centre of the whole length of the buns.

Bake for 35 minutes (25 - 30 mins for small buns) or until golden brown and the tops are firm. Allow to cool on the tray before slicing and serving.

To serve: Cut a V shape in the pre-cut line down the centre of the buns and remove the small wedge of bread and place your fillings into the cavity.

Suitable to freeze (if you would like to crispen them back up, place the buns into a preheated oven for 5 - 10 minutes).

Irish Potato Scones (egg-free)

Potato scones or fried potato patties are native to Ireland and Scotland. I've used the purple/red skin sweet potato with white flesh to make a Paleo friendly version. These scones make a great side dish for breakfast with bacon and eggs. They are delicious topped with fermented chutney for a savoury snack. Leftover scones can be sliced in half and toasted, then filled and eaten like a sandwich.

Makes: 12   Prep time: 15 mins   Cooking time: 20 mins

Ingredients

500g purple/red skin sweet potato (white flesh), peel and dice

3 Tbsp canned coconut cream, to mash the sweet potato

250g (2¼ cups) almond meal/flour (from blanched almonds)

85g (⅔ cup) arrowroot flour

2 tsp baking powder (gluten free)

¾ tsp fine sea salt

2 Tbsp ghee, for cooking

Directions

Add the peeled and diced sweet potato to a medium saucepan of boiling water. Cook, simmering for 10 - 15 minutes or until tender (I dice the potato small to shorten the cooking time).

Meanwhile, add the almond meal, arrowroot, baking powder and salt to a large bowl. Mix well to combine and to remove any lumps.

Drain the cooked sweet potato using a sieve, and then return it to the pot. Add the coconut cream and mash the potato well (this potato doesn't mash soft like regular sweet potato, it's a firm drier texture).

Add the still warm mashed potato to the dry ingredients and mix through well with your hands to create a smooth soft dough. Allow to sit for 5 minutes (this helps the dough become less sticky).

Divide the dough into 12 portions. Take a ball of dough and flatten between your palms to create a 7cm round patty, 5 - 6mm thick (the scones will rise slightly when cooking). Repeat with the remaining dough portions.

Heat a large frying pan on medium heat. Add ½ a tablespoon of ghee and swirl over the base of the pan. Add half the round patties and cook for 5 minutes or until golden brown. Turn over and cook the second side for 4 - 5 minutes, adding another ½ tablespoon of ghee. Once cooked, transfer to a cooling rack. Repeat with the remaining patties.

Serve warm with bacon and eggs for breakfast or at room temperature spread with grass-fed butter or ghee. Serve with stews to scoop up the gravy or dipped into soup.

Hot Cross Buns

Hot Cross Buns have always been a tradition at Easter time in our home. Baking these tasty grain-free, spiced buns, your family definitely won't miss the gluten and additive packed commercial ones.

Makes: 10   Prep time: 25 mins   Cooking time: 25 mins

Ingredients

3 large eggs
1 sml – med ripe banana
60ml (¼ cup) macadamia nut oil
3 Tbsp unprocessed honey
1 tsp apple cider vinegar
250g (2¼ cups) almond meal/flour
128g (1 cup) arrowroot flour or tapioca
2 Tbsp psyllium husk powder
1 Tbsp fine orange zest

1 Tbsp cinnamon
2 tsp mixed spice
½ tsp nutmeg
1 tsp baking powder (gluten free)
1 tsp baking soda (bicarb)
¼ tsp fine sea salt
½ cup sultanas (organic)
4 large Medjool dates, pitted and diced

CROSSES:
3 Tbsp arrowroot flour
2 Tbsp almond meal
1¼ - 1½ Tbsp filtered water

GLAZE:
1 Tbsp honey
1 Tbsp filtered water
¼ tsp cinnamon

Directions

Preheat oven to 170c (fan-forced). Line a baking tray with baking paper.

Add the eggs, banana, oil, honey and vinegar to a food processor. Process for 10 seconds or until combined.

Add the almond meal, arrowroot, psyllium powder, zest, spices, baking powder, soda and salt to the wet ingredients. Process for 5 seconds, scrape down sides of the bowl and then process for a further 15 seconds.

Remove the blade and use a spatula to mix the sultanas and dates evenly through the mixture. Allow the mixture to sit for 5 minutes to thicken further.

Scoop out 10 equal portions of the mixture using a spatula and place onto the prepared tray. Leave a slight gap between each portion (they will rise and fill the space when cooking). Use damp fingers to smooth and shape the portions to look like buns.

Bake for 15 - 18 minutes or until risen and just starting to lightly brown. Remove buns from the oven and pipe over the crosses (see notes below) and return to bake for a further 10 minutes or until lightly golden and a skewer inserted comes out clean. (The inside will be a little darker in colour than store-bought buns, we have delicious spices in these buns).

To make the crosses: You need a thick paste. Add the arrowroot and almond meal to a small bowl and stir. Add 1 tablespoon of water and mix well, then add extra water by the teaspoon to create a thick paste. Spoon into a piping bag. Pipe lengthways in one continuous line over the buns and then across (cover the end to stop the paste dripping as you change direction).

Glazing the buns (optional): Glazing makes the buns shine and look more like shop bought but not necessary. Heat the honey, water and cinnamon together. Once the buns have cooled slightly, use a pastry brush to add a thin coat of syrup.

Serve warm with grass-fed butter or ghee. They are also delicious sliced and toasted. The buns freeze well, just warm before serving.

SAVOURY BREADS

Garlic and Rosemary Focaccia

Focaccia is a flat oven-baked Italian bread. This garlicky bread is soft inside and crisp on the outside. It's perfect to use for sandwiches, as an appetizer or for sopping up sauces and dipping into olive oil mixed with balsamic vinegar.

Serves: 6 - 8   **Prep time:** 15 mins   **Cooking time:** 25 mins

Ingredients

110g (1 cup) almond meal/flour (from blanched almonds)

42g (⅓ cup) arrowroot flour or tapioca

26g (¼ cup) coconut flour, sifted

2 Tbsp golden flaxseed meal

2 Tbsp nutritional yeast flakes (aka savoury flakes)

½ tsp baking soda (bicarb)

½ tsp sea salt

4 large eggs

125ml (½ cup) canned coconut milk (a thick brand like Ayam)

60g (¼ cup) ghee or grass-fed butter, melted and cooled

2 tsp apple cider vinegar

1 tsp maple syrup (optional)

½ tsp garlic, minced

TOPPING:

3 Tbsp rosemary leaves, roughly chopped

1 tsp garlic, minced

3 Tbsp ghee, melted and warm

Coarse sea salt or flakes

Directions

Preheat oven to 190c (fan-forced). Line a 32 x 18cm slice tin with baking paper (grease the tin before adding the paper to keep the paper in place).

Add the almond meal, arrowroot, coconut flour, flaxseed, nutritional yeast flakes, baking soda and salt to a large bowl and stir well to mix.

In a medium bowl, whisk together the eggs, coconut milk, ghee, apple cider vinegar, maple syrup and garlic.

Pour the wet ingredients into the bowl containing the dry ingredients and stir well to create a smooth batter. Spoon the batter into the prepared tin and level the surface (I find it's easier to use damp fingers to spread the batter). Let sit for 5 – 8 minutes.

Add the topping ingredients except for the salt, into a small bowl and mix together. Spoon the topping mixture over the batter and spread evenly with a spatula (the ghee needs to be warm so it doesn't become firm before you finish spreading it). Sprinkle over a little salt.

Bake for 25 minutes or until golden and crisp on top and bread is coming away from the sides. Allow to sit for 5 - 10 minutes then remove by lifting the baking paper.

Cut into squares or slices and serve warm.

Pumpkin and Thyme Bread

This savoury pumpkin bread is so tasty, it's lovely and moist and packed with nutrients. Enjoy warm with soup, toasted or it's ideal for dipping into olive oil for a healthy snack.

Makes: 1 loaf **Prep time:** 20 mins **Cooking time:** 60 mins

---

Ingredients

275g (2½ cups) almond meal/flour (from blanched almonds)

60g (½ cup) golden flaxseed meal

42g (⅓ cup) arrowroot flour or tapioca

1 tsp cinnamon

½ tsp cumin

1 tsp baking soda (bicarb)

½ tsp fine sea salt

3 tsp thyme leaves or 1 tsp dried thyme leaves

4 large eggs

60ml (¼ cup) macadamia oil or mild olive oil

1 Tbsp apple cider vinegar

2 tsp 100% maple syrup

160g (1½ cups) pumpkin, grated

Pumpkin seeds (pepitas) to sprinkle on top

Directions

Preheat oven to 160c (fan-forced). Line a 21 x 10cm loaf tin with baking paper.

Add the almond meal, flaxseed, arrowroot, cinnamon, cumin, baking soda, salt and thyme to a large bowl. Stir to mix well.

Add the eggs, oil, vinegar and maple syrup to a medium bowl and whisk together to combine.

Pour the egg mixture into the dry ingredients and stir well to combine. Add the grated pumpkin and mix well to distribute evenly without delay before the mixture starts to thicken (I find it's best to use my hands to push the grated pumpkin through the mixture).

Transfer the mixture into the prepared tin. Use damp fingers to press the batter down evenly into the tin. Sprinkle the top with pumpkin seeds and gently press so they stick to the bread.

Bake for 60 - 65 minutes or until a skewer inserted comes out clean and the top is crisp.

Allow to sit in the tin for 15 minutes before removing to finish cooling on a wire rack.

Store in an airtight container in the fridge for up to 5 days.

Carrot and Parsnip Muffins

You get a good serve of vegetables in these muffins. The root vegetables and basil give a savoury, sweet flavour and they create a lovely soft texture. Serve warm for a light lunch or with a bowl of soup. You may also like to add some diced cooked bacon.

Makes: 12   **Prep time:** 20 mins   **Cooking time:** 45 mins

---

Ingredients

220g (2 cups) almond meal/flour (from blanched almonds)

26g (¼ cup) coconut flour

33g (¼ cup) arrowroot flour or tapioca

3 Tbsp nutritional yeast flakes (aka savoury flakes)

1½ tsp paprika

¾ tsp baking soda (bicarb)

¾ tsp fine sea salt

4 large eggs

125ml almond milk or milk of choice

60ml (¼ cup) macadamia oil

⅓ cup fresh basil leaves, roughly chopped

2 spring onions with some green tops, sliced

200g (1 lge) carrot, grated

200g (1 lge) parsnip, grated

Directions

Preheat oven to 170c (fan-forced). Place paper liners in a large muffin tin, this will prevent the muffins sticking or use a silicon muffin tray.

Add the almond meal, coconut flour, arrowroot flour, nutritional yeast flakes, paprika, baking soda, and salt to a food processor. Process for 15 seconds to combine and create a fine texture.

Add the eggs, milk and oil. Process for 10 - 12 seconds to combine all the ingredients.

Add the basil and spring onions, pulse a few times to blend evenly through the mixture. Transfer the mixture to a large bowl and add the grated carrot and parsnip. Stir well to distribute the vegetables evenly through the mixture (if you are using bacon add at this time).

Spoon the mixture into the prepared muffin tin and smooth the tops. Bake for 45 minutes or until firm to the touch and golden.

Serve warm or at room temperature with ghee or grass-fed butter. Suitable to freeze.

Breadsticks

I've flavoured these crispy breadsticks with garlic and basil. You will find they are perfect on their own as a snack or as an appetizer to scoop up a sauce or dip.

Makes: 8   **Prep time:** 20 mins   **Cooking time:** 20 mins

---

Ingredients

110g (1 cup) almond meal/flour (from blanched almonds)

2 Tbsp coconut flour

2 Tbsp arrowroot flour or tapioca

¾ tsp dried basil

½ tsp garlic powder

½ tsp baking powder (gluten free)

½ tsp fine sea salt, plus extra for sprinkling

1 large egg

2 Tbsp olive oil

1 tsp 100% maple syrup

Olive oil for rolling the dough

Directions

Preheat oven to 180c (fan-forced). Line a baking tray with baking paper.

Add the almond meal, coconut flour, arrowroot, basil, garlic, baking powder and salt to a large bowl. Stir well to combine and remove any lumps.

Whisk the egg, oil and maple syrup together in a small bowl and pour into the dry ingredients. Stir well, and then use your hands to bring the dough together. Allow to sit for 5 minutes to take up some moisture.

Divide the dough into 8 equal portions on a sheet of baking paper. Coat your hands with olive oil, take a portion and using your fingers shape the dough into a rough sausage. Use an oiled palm to gently roll out the dough to a 16cm stick. If you find the dough cracks while rolling, just press together with your fingers to mend.

Place the sticks onto the prepared tray and use your fingers to brush the tops and sides with a little extra olive oil and add a light sprinkle of sea salt.

Bake for 20 minutes or until golden and very crisp. Allow to cool on the tray before serving.

Store in an airtight glass container to keep them crisp.

FLATBREADS, TORTILLAS and PIZZA BASES

Naan Bread (egg-free)

Naan bread is a perfect accompaniment to dishes like Indian Butter Chicken. This isn't exactly like traditional Naan bread but it's a delicious paleo version, it's crisp on the outside and soft in the middle and adored by my family.

Makes: 6   **Prep time:** 10 mins   **Cooking time:** 20 mins

Ingredients

110g (1 cup) almond meal/flour (from blanched almonds)

65g (½ cup) arrowroot flour or tapioca

2 tsp psyllium husks

½ tsp fine sea salt

125ml (½ cup) canned coconut milk (use a thick brand like Ayam)

160ml (⅔ cup) filtered water (use less water if your coconut milk is watery)

Ghee for frying

Directions

Add the almond meal, arrowroot, psyllium and salt to a bowl and stir to combine.

Pour in the coconut milk and water. Use an electric handheld beater on low–medium and beat to produce a smooth mixture (a wire whisk can also be used, make sure to remove all the lumps). Allow to sit for 5 – 8 minutes to thicken.

Heat one or two small non-stick frying pans or crepe pans on medium heat. I like to use two pans to halve the time it takes to cook the bread or you could use a large 32cm pan and cook a couple in one pan).

Add ½ teaspoon of ghee to coat the pan. Pour ¼ of a cup of batter into the heated pan. Make a circle with a diameter of approximately 12cm, you can use the back of a spoon to push out and spread the batter if needed.

Cook the first side for approximately 4 minutes or until the bottom is golden brown and crisp. The batter should bubble a little while cooking (don't be tempted to turn over too soon, you want a crisp outside to the bread). Cook the second side for 3 minutes and add another ½ teaspoon of ghee to the pan each time you flip the bread or as needed.

Lay the cooked Naan bread out on a wire rack in a single layer or if you prefer to keep it warm then spread out on a tray in the oven while cooking the remaining batter.

Optional: serve spread with a little ghee or plain.

Garlic Coconut Flour Naan Bread (nut & egg-free)

This is a nut-free version of my Naan bread recipe but with a twist, I've added garlic but it is optional. The bread also works well if you require a nut and egg free wrap, just add extra water to make a thinner batter.

Makes: 7   Prep time: 10 mins   Cooking time: 20 mins

Ingredients

35g (⅓ cup) coconut flour, sifted

42g (⅓ cup) arrowroot flour or tapioca

2 tsp psyllium husks

¾ tsp fine sea salt

1½ tsp garlic, minced

250ml (1 cup) canned coconut milk (use a thick brand like Ayam)

180ml (¾ cup) filtered water (use less water if your milk is watery)

Ghee for frying

Optional, spread with a little ghee, garlic, and chopped parsley when serving

Directions

Sift the coconut flour into a bowl, add the arrowroot, psyllium husks and salt and stir to combine.

Add the garlic, coconut milk and water. Use an electric handheld beater on low–medium and beat to produce a smooth mixture (a wire whisk can also be used, make sure to remove all the lumps). This is a very thick batter.

Heat one or two small non-stick frying pans or crepe pans on medium heat. (I like to use two pans to halve the time it takes to cook the bread or you could use a large 32cm pan and cook a couple in one pan).

Add ½ teaspoon of ghee to coat the pan. Pour ¼ of a cup of batter into the heated pan. Use the back of a spoon to push the batter out and spread to make a circle with a diameter of approximately 12cm.

Cook the first side for approximately 4 minutes or until the bottom is golden and firm. The top should have risen a little and the wet shiny look has gone when it's ready to turn. Use a large spatula to turn the bread. Cook the second side for 3 - 4 minutes and add a further ½ teaspoon of ghee to the pan each time you flip the bread or as needed.

Lay the cooked naan bread out on a wire rack in a single layer or if you prefer to keep it warm then spread out on a tray in the oven while cooking the remaining batter.

Tortillas (egg-free)

These Paleo tortillas fold in half nicely and are firm enough to hold your filling when they are freshly cooked. If you would like flexible soft tortillas to roll up, let them cool covered with a tea towel. This recipe is so versatile.

Makes: 8 **Prep time:** 10 mins **Cooking time:** 30 mins

Ingredients

110g (1 cup) almond meal/flour (from blanched almonds)

65g (½ cup) arrowroot flour or tapioca

¾ tsp fine sea salt

250ml (1 cup) filtered water

80ml (⅓ cup) canned coconut milk (use a thick brand like Ayam)

2 Tbsp olive oil

Ghee for cooking

Directions

Add the almond meal, arrowroot and salt to a large bowl. Mix well to break up any lumps.

Add the water, coconut milk and olive oil. Whisk or use an electric handheld beater to mix well, making sure to remove any clumps in the mixture. Set aside for 5 minutes.

Heat a small 20 – 24cm non-stick frying pan or crepe pan on medium–low heat (I use 2 pans to cook the tortillas in half the time). Add ¼ - ½ teaspoon of ghee.

Pour a ¼-measuring cup full of the mixture into the centre of the heated pan or pans. The mixture should bubble and spread out into a circle. Cook the first side for approximately 3 - 4 minutes, don't allow the mixture to get overly crisp, otherwise the edges may crack when you fold the tortilla. Flip using a wide spatula once the bottom is firm and cook the second side for approximately 2 minutes. Repeat until all the mixture is cooked. Add a little extra ghee to the pan between each addition.

Place the cooked tortillas on a cooling rack to keep them firm, they are best served straight away (if needed, you can crispen them up in a hot oven by placing the tortillas in a single layer on a baking tray for 8 – 10 minutes or pop them back into the frying pan).

Nut 'n' Egg Free Wraps

(nut & egg-free)

Use these wraps to hold your sandwich fillings in. They are suitable for school lunch boxes, as they contain no nuts or eggs.

Makes: 6 - 7   **Prep time:** 10 mins   **Cooking time:** 20 mins

---

Ingredients

60g (¼ cup) sunflower butter or hulled tahini

42g (⅓ cup) arrowroot flour or tapioca

1 Tbsp psyllium husks

½ tsp fine sea salt

½ tsp smoked paprika (helps with savoury flavour)

200ml coconut milk (a thick brand like Ayam)

125ml warm water, plus extra if needed

Coconut oil or ghee for cooking

Directions

Add the sunflower butter or tahini to a large bowl (stir in the jar before adding to prevent the extra oil on top going into the recipe) then add the arrowroot, psyllium husks, salt, smoked paprika and coconut milk. Beat with a hand-held electric beater to produce a smooth mixture.

Pour in the warm water and continue beating to create a smooth batter. If needed, add a little extra water if the batter thickens. The batter needs to be able to spread out in the pan to create a 16 – 17cm circle.

Heat a crepe pan or small frying pan on medium-low heat. Smear a little coconut oil over the pan (I use two pans to save time).

Pour a ¼ cup of the batter into the heated pan and swirl quickly to spread out. Cook for 2 – 3 minutes on each side. Use a large spatula to turn the wraps. Reduce the heat if the wraps start to brown too quickly, you don't want the wraps to be very crisp, as they need to be able to roll up.

Place the cooked wraps in a single layer on a wire rack to cool (if you stack them on top of each other they will sweat and become too soft).

Crepes

These crepes have a lovely soft texture and roll up perfectly. The arrowroot flour/starch holds them together and makes the crepes flexible. Arrowroot is the easiest starch to digest and is often used for stomach issues. Omit the vanilla if you are filling the crepes with a savoury food.

Makes: 6   **Prep time:** 10 mins   **Cooking time:** 10 mins

Ingredients

140g (1¼ cups) almond meal/flour (from blanched almonds)

85g (⅔ cup) arrowroot flour

¼ tsp fine sea salt

310ml (1¼ cups) almond or cashew milk (or milk of choice)

1 large egg

2 tsp 100% maple syrup

2 tsp vanilla extract (organic)

Ghee for cooking

Directions

Add the almond meal, arrowroot flour and salt to a large bowl and mix to combine and remove any lumps.

Add the milk, egg, maple syrup and vanilla. Beat on low using a hand-held electric beater, then increase speed to medium (or a metal whisk can be used). Allow the mixture to sit for a few minutes before starting to cook.

Heat a small 20cm non-stick crepe or frying pan on medium-low heat. Wipe the pan over with a small amount of ghee. Lift the heated pan from the stove and pour a ⅓ of a cup of mixture over the pan and swirl it straight away to spread the batter evenly over the whole pan (if you find it's not spreading well, reduce the heat).

Cook the first side for approximately 2 minutes, the bottom of the crepe should still be soft and pliable (not crisp). Turn over using a large spatula and cook the second side for 1 – 2 minutes. Add a little ghee between cooking each crepe. Set the crepes aside covered while cooking the remaining mixture.

Serve filled with fruit and dairy-free cream for dessert or omit the vanilla in the recipe and serve filled with leftovers or sausage and egg for breakfast. (My favourite is sliced strawberries and mango with whipped cashew cream or coconut yoghurt and a sprinkle of cinnamon).

Coriander and Garlic Flatbread

Flatbread is generally used to accompany dishes that have a sauce or gravy for dipping, but this delicious recipe is also perfect on its own. Drizzle the flatbread with a little avocado oil and chopped coriander leaves. I also have an option for those allergic to nuts and egg, see notes below.

Makes: 8   **Prep time:** 15 mins   **Cooking time:** 15 mins

Ingredients

220g (2 cups) almond meal/flour (from blanched almonds)

95g (¾ cup) arrowroot flour or tapioca

½ tsp baking soda (bicarb)

½ tsp fine sea salt

125ml (½ cup) canned coconut milk (a thick brand like Ayam)

125ml (½ cup) filtered water

1 Tbsp avocado oil or olive oil

1 large egg, lightly beaten

1 tsp minced garlic

¼ cup chopped coriander leaves

Directions

Preheat oven to 180c (fan-forced) and line two baking trays with baking paper.

Add the almond meal, arrowroot, baking soda and salt to a large bowl. Stir to mix and remove any lumps.

Pour the coconut milk and filtered water into the dry ingredients (if your coconut milk is watery, use a little less filtered water or replace milk with cream). Whisk or stir well to remove any clumps in the mixture.

Add the oil and beaten egg and mix well to produce a smooth thick batter. Add the garlic and coriander and stir to distribute them evenly through the batter.

Add four equal portions of the batter to each lined tray. Roughly two heaped tablespoons for each of the eight portions of flatbread. Use the back of a spoon to flatten and spread out the batter into rounds, approximately 11 - 12cms in diameter.

Bake for 15 minutes or until the tops are firm and bottoms are lightly brown (there will only be a slight colour change on top).

Serve drizzled with avocado oil and a sprinkling of chopped coriander leaves.

Nut and Egg Free Version: Swap the almond meal with ground sunflower seeds made into a fine meal. Use 1½ teaspoons of baking powder in place of the soda/bicarb (baking soda and sunflower seeds together react and the mixture turns green, it's fine to eat just looks funny). You can omit the egg and increase the coconut milk, roughly 3 tablespoons extra.

Crispy Spinach Flatbread

(egg-free)

This flatbread is so crisp that you can make yummy chips out of it for dips and nachos. They are a perfect size for an individual serve and can be used to dip in and scoop up your meal, but best of all they are a delicious savoury snack when you need some crunch (the dough is very green from the spinach but once cooked it changes).

Makes: 6   **Prep time:** 20 mins   **Cooking time:** 30 mins

Ingredients

50g (1½ cups) baby spinach, firmly packed
Boiling water for soaking the spinach
2 Tbsp golden flaxseed meal
4 Tbsp filtered water for soaking the flaxseed
140g (1¼ cups) almond meal/flour
42g (⅓ cup) arrowroot flour or tapioca
2 Tbsp sesame seeds

½ tsp fine sea salt or to taste
½ tsp paprika
¼ tsp onion powder
¼ tsp garlic powder
Ghee for frying or coconut oil

Directions

Place the spinach into a heatproof container. Pour the boiling water over the spinach and cover. Set aside to soften and wilt for 5 - 10 minutes.

Add the flaxseed and water to a small bowl and stir. Let sit for 5 minutes to thicken.

Drain the spinach into a sieve and press down firmly with the back of a spoon to remove all the liquid.

Add the spinach, flaxseed mixture, almond meal, arrowroot, sesame seeds, salt and spices to a food processor. Process until the dough comes together and forms a ball.

Remove the dough and using kitchen scales, weigh out 5 x 60g size balls of dough. Place a ball of dough between 2 sheets of baking paper and roll out to make a 16cm circle. I use a small saucepan lid as a cookie cutter (it's so easy as you can lift it off using the handle), or you can use a 15cm saucer to cut around. Remove the excess trimmings and put them aside, you will have enough excess dough at the end to make the 6th circle. After cutting each circle, place them on a sheet of paper (it's an easy dough to handle).

Heat a small non-stick frying pan on medium heat (I use two pans to save time). Add a ¼ teaspoon of ghee to coat the pan. Lift a piece of rolled dough off the baking paper and place in the pan. Cook for 3 minutes on each side or until lightly brown and crisp. Repeat with the remaining circles and add ghee as needed.

Cool the cooked flatbread on a wire rack in a single layer. Once cooled you can break up into corn chip size pieces for using with dips or as a snack.

Store in a glass airtight container to keep them crisp.

Pizza Bases

This is a no-fuss recipe that tastes delicious and has a great texture the whole family will love. The bases freeze well, so make double to keep some on hand for a quick weekend meal. I've made the pizza bases into individual serving sizes.

Serves: 4   Prep time: 10 mins   Cooking time: 10 mins

Ingredients

110g (1 cup) almond meal/flour

95g (¾ cup) arrowroot or tapioca flour, plus extra for dusting your hands

35g (⅓ cup) coconut flour

¾ tsp Italian herbs/seasoning

¾ tsp fine sea salt

½ tsp baking soda (bicarb)

2 large eggs

3 Tbsp avocado oil

2 tsp apple cider vinegar or lemon juice

60ml (¼ cup) filtered water

Directions

Preheat oven to 190c (fan-forced) and line 2 large baking trays with baking paper.

Add the almond meal, arrowroot, coconut flour, Italian herbs, salt and baking soda to a large bowl. Stir to break up any lumps and to combine the flours well.

Add the eggs, oil and vinegar to a small bowl and whisk. Pour into the flour mixture and mix well. Add the water and mix well to combine. Allow the dough to sit for 5 minutes to soak up some of the moisture. The dough will be sticky.

Place 2 – 3 tablespoons of arrowroot flour on a small plate for coating your hands. Divide the dough into 4 equal portions, dust your hands well and roll each portion into a ball.

Place 2 balls, well spaced, onto each prepared tray. With well-dusted hands, start from the centre and work the dough out with your fingers to a thin 17cm (6.5in) round.

Bake for 8 - 10 minutes (don't over cook as the base will go back into the oven with the toppings).

Top the bases with your favourite toppings and place back into the oven until they are cooked through.

Sweet Potato Pizza Base
(nut & egg-free)

This pizza base is made especially for those with intolerances or allergies to nuts and eggs. No one should miss out on pizza night! This base is full of healthy fibre and will surely fill your hungry children. You can also make Focaccia Bread out of this recipe, see notes below.

Serves: 4 - 6 **Prep time:** 15 mins **Cooking time:** 20 mins

Ingredients

70g (⅔ cup) coconut flour, sifted

30g (¼ cup) golden flaxseed meal

¾ tsp Italian herbs

¼ tsp garlic powder

¼ tsp onion powder

½ tsp fine sea salt

1½ cups mashed sweet potato, cooled (1 lge 480-500g sweet potato)

2 Tbsp olive or avocado oil

Directions

Preheat oven to 190c (fan-forced). Line a large pizza tray with baking paper (grease the tray to prevent the paper sliding when you are spreading the dough out).

Add the coconut flour, flaxseed, Italian herbs, garlic powder, onion powder and salt to a large bowl and stir well.

Add the mashed sweet potato and oil to the dry ingredients and mix well to incorporate all the ingredients to create a smooth dough. Use clean hands to form the dough into a ball.

Place the dough onto the prepared tray and press the ball down to flatten into a circle. Use your fingers to push the dough out from the centre to create a 30cm circle with a thickness of 0.5cm. Smooth and neaten the edges.

Bake the pizza base for 20 minutes.

Meanwhile, prepare your toppings and add them to a bowl. Pour over a little olive oil, Italian herbs, salt and pepper, and mix to coat all the ingredients.

Once the pizza base is cooked, spread over 4 tablespoons of tomato paste and I like to lay some greens over it (I use baby spinach) then add your prepared toppings. Bake for 10 - 15 minutes or unto the topping ingredients are cooked to your liking.

To serve: add dollops of nut 'cheese' spread or mashed avocado and basil leaves.

To make Focaccia Bread: Add 1½ teaspoons of baking powder with the dry ingredients. Shape the dough out into a rectangle with a thickness of 1cm. For a topping: add 2 – 3 tablespoons of olive oil, 2 tablespoons of chopped rosemary leaves and 1 teaspoon of minced garlic to a small bowl and mix. Spread the topping out evenly over the dough. Bake for 25 minutes or until cooked through and golden on the top.

CRACKERS

Rosemary and Seed Crackers (egg-free)

These crisp and tasty crackers are delicious eaten plain or used with dips and spreads. They stay crisp and fresh stored in an airtight glass container for up to 2 weeks. By making your own crackers you get to avoid the additives that are found in many commercial brands.

Makes: 50 **Prep time:** 20 mins **Cooking time:** 20 mins

Ingredients

110g (1 cup) almond meal/flour (from blanched almonds)

140g (1 cup) cashews

3 Tbsp coconut flour

70g (½ cup) sesame seeds

50g (⅓ cup) pumpkin seeds (pepitas)

50g (⅓ cup) sunflower seeds

30g (¼ cup) golden flaxseed meal

1¼ tsp fine sea salt, plus extra to sprinkle on top

1 large sprig rosemary, leaves removed and chopped

3 Tbsp macadamia oil

80ml filtered water

Directions

Preheat oven to 160c (fan-forced). You will need 2 - 3 large baking trays (it will depend on the size of your trays) and 3 - 4 pieces of baking paper the size of the trays.

Add the almond meal, cashews and coconut flour to a food processor. Process for 10 seconds or until the cashews have ground down to the fine texture of a nut meal.

Add the sesame seeds, pumpkin seeds, sunflower seeds, flaxseed meal and salt.

Add the rosemary, oil and water to the mixture and process for approximately 10 - 12 seconds to mix well and form a dough. (The flaxseed will start to soak up the moisture, if you find the dough starts to get a bit too firm before rolling, wet your hands and kneed the moisture in).

Divide the dough into two portions and place one between 2 sheets of the baking paper. Use a rolling pin to roll out the dough into a rectangle that's approximately 2 - 3mm thick. Remove the top sheet of paper and slide the bottom sheet containing the rolled dough onto a baking tray. Use a pizza cutter or sharp knife to cut vertical and horizontal lines through the dough, creating 5cm squares. Repeat with the remaining dough. Sprinkle a little extra sea salt over the cut dough.

Bake for 20 - 25 minutes or until lightly golden and firm (turn the tray once while cooking for even colour). Allow to cool on the trays for 15 minutes, then separate the crackers by snapping them apart.

Store in an airtight glass container for up to 2 weeks.

Sesame Crackers

These light and crispy crackers are perfect for dipping into dips and spreading with pate.

Makes: 34 – 36   **Prep Time:** 15 mins   **Cooking time:** 20 mins

---

Ingredients

220g (2 cups) almond meal/flour (from blanched almonds)

42g (⅓ cup) arrowroot flour or tapioca

2 Tbsp sesame seeds

2 tsp mustard powder

½ tsp baking soda (bicarb)

½ tsp fine sea salt

1 large egg

2 tsp filtered water

Extra sesame seeds and salt for sprinkling on top

Directions

Preheat oven to 160c (fan-forced).

Add the almond meal, arrowroot, sesame seeds, mustard powder, baking soda and salt to a food processor. Process for 8 – 10 seconds to produce a fine texture.

Add the egg and filtered water and process until a dough starts to form (approximately 10 seconds). Remove from the processor and give the dough a quick knead to combine well.

Place the dough between 2 sheets of baking paper. Use a rolling pin to roll the dough out to a very thin 1.5 - 2mm rectangle. Remove the top sheet of paper and trim so you have straight edges. Set trimmings aside to be rerolled.

Slide the sheet of paper containing the rolled dough onto a baking tray and sprinkle with sesame seeds and salt. Place a clean sheet of paper over the dough and gently smooth your hands over the surface to lightly press the seeds into the dough. Use a pizza cutter or large knife to cut vertical and horizontal lines through the dough, creating 5cm squares.

Bake for approximately 20 minutes or until lightly golden and crisp.

Store in an airtight container to keep the crackers crisp.

Sunflower and Poppy Seed Crackers (nut & egg-free)

These nut-free crackers are perfect to add your favourite toppings to. They also work brilliantly for lunches, add your filling and pop a cracker on top to make a cracker sandwich.

Makes: 22   **Prep time:** 15 mins   **Cooking time:** 20 mins

---

Ingredients

150g (1 cup) sunflower seeds

85g (⅔ cup) arrowroot or tapioca flour

38g (¼ cup) sesame seeds

30g (¼ cup) golden flaxseed meal

1 tsp fine sea salt

¾ tsp baking powder (gluten free)

1 Tbsp poppy seeds

80ml filtered water

3 Tbsp olive oil

Directions

Preheat oven to 160c (fan-forced). You will need 2 large baking trays and 3 pieces of baking paper the size of your trays.

Add the sunflower seeds, arrowroot, sesame seeds, flaxseed, salt and baking powder to a food processor. Process for approximately 20 seconds to reach a fine flour texture.

Add the poppy seeds, water and oil. Process to moisten and bring the mixture together (approx. 8 – 10 seconds). Remove the blade and scoop out the mixture with your hands and squeeze between your palms to combine well into a ball of dough.

Divide the dough in half, place one portion between 2 sheets of the baking paper. Use a rolling pin to roll out the dough into a rectangle, 2mm thick. Remove the top sheet of paper and use a pizza cutter or sharp knife to trim and straighten the outer edges. Cut into cracker shapes approximately 6 x 10cm, then slide the bottom sheet containing the cut dough onto a baking tray. Repeat with the remaining dough and the trimmings.

Bake for 20 – 25 minutes until lightly golden and crisp (turn the tray once while cooking for an even colour). Allow to cool on the trays for 15 minutes.

Serve with your favourite toppings, they are also delicious plain or spread with grass-fed butter.

Store in an airtight glass container for up to 10 days.

Romano Cheese Crackers

These delicious and tasty cheese crackers are my grandkids all time favourites. They contain aged Romano cheese, avoid if you don't tolerate dairy (matured cheese loses lactose as it ages).

Makes: approx. 50 **Prep time:** 20 mins **Cooking time:** 20 mins (Contains dairy)

Ingredients

330g (3 cups) almond meal/flour (from blanched almonds)

2 tsp dry mustard powder

½ tsp fine salt salt

½ tsp baking soda (bicarb)

1 cup Romano cheese, grated (or any tasty aged cheese of your choice)

3 Tbsp macadamia oil (or mild flavoured olive oil)

2 large eggs

Directions

Preheat oven to 160c (fan-forced). You will need 3 large baking trays and 4 pieces of baking paper the size of the trays.

Add the almond meal, mustard, salt, baking soda and cheese to a large bowl. Mix well to combine and remove any lumps.

Add the oil and eggs to a medium bowl and whisk together. Pour the wet ingredients into the almond meal mixture and combine well. Knead the dough gently for a few seconds.

Divide the dough into thirds. Place one portion of dough between 2 sheets of baking paper. Use a rolling pin to roll the dough out to a thin rectangle, approx. 2 – 3 mm thick. Remove the top piece of paper and slide the bottom piece of baking paper with the rolled-out dough onto a baking tray. Cut the dough into 4cm squares using a pizza cutter or knife. Repeat process with the remaining dough.

Bake each tray for approx. 20 minutes or until lightly golden and crisp. Let the crackers cool on the trays for 15 minutes, then break-up the crackers along the cut lines.

Store in an airtight glass container for up to 10 days.

NOTE: If you find the outer crackers are golden but centre ones need extra cooking time. Remove from oven and allow to cool a little, then break off the outer crackers and place the remaining ones back into the oven to cook a little longer.

Apricot and Rosemary Toasts

Apricot and Rosemary Toasts (aka Melba toast) are perfect for your antipasto platter. Serve with an assortment of pickled vegetables, olives and pate. The toasts are baked twice to create a crispy cracker. (Dried figs also work really well in this recipe).

Makes: 24 slices   **Prep time:** 20 mins   **Cooking time:** 50 mins

---

Ingredients

165g (1½ cups) almond meal/flour (from blanched almonds)

65g (½ cup) arrowroot flour or tapioca

40g (¼ cup) sunflower seeds, plus 2 extra tablespoons

40g (¼ cup) pumpkin seeds (pepitas), plus 2 extra tablespoons

1 Tbsp poppy seeds, plus 1 extra teaspoon

1½ tsp baking powder (gluten free)

½ tsp fine sea salt

2 large eggs

3 tsp dried rosemary

60g organic dried apricots or figs, diced (sulphur free)

Directions

Preheat oven to 170c (fan-forced). Line a 21 x 10cm loaf tin with baking paper, also line 2 baking trays and set aside.

Add the almond meal, arrowroot, sunflowers, pumpkin seeds, poppy seeds, baking powder and salt to a food processor. Process for 15 seconds to produce a finer texture.

Add the eggs and rosemary and process for approximately 8 – 10 seconds until the dough starts to gather together.

Sprinkle the extra sunflowers, pumpkin seeds and poppy seeds, and the chopped apricots evenly around the bowl. Pulse several times to mix them through the dough but not to break them up.

Scoop the dough into the prepared tin, use your fingers to press the dough firmly down and smooth the top.

Bake for 25 – 30 minutes or until the bread is lightly brown on top. Remove the baked bread from the tin and allow it to cool on a wire rack for 15 minutes.

Place the bread onto a chopping board while it's still warm and slice very thinly using a bread knife. Slice slowly to prevent the edges crumbling and slice no thicker than 0.5cms. Place the slices on their side on the prepared baking tray.

Bake the slices at 170c for 25 - 30 minutes or until they start to lightly brown and become crisp. Allow to cool on the trays.

Store in a glass airtight container to keep them crisp for up to 10 days.

PASTRY

Sausage Roll Pastry (egg-free)

I've nicknamed this egg-free pastry 'Sausage Roll Pastry', as it rolls perfectly without cracking or splitting. It's so easy to work with and it's not only perfect for making sausage rolls but it works for pasties and vegetable triangles.

Makes: 1 batch/530g **Prep time:** 15 mins **Cooking time:** 25 mins

Ingredients

140g (1¼ cups) almond meal/flour (from blanched almonds

128g (1 cup) arrowroot or tapioca flour

3 Tbsp coconut flour

3 Tbsp golden flaxseed, fine ground

¾ tsp baking soda (bicarb)

½ tsp fine sea salt

200g natural coconut yoghurt (or Greek yoghurt)

Melted ghee to brush over pastry or 1 egg beaten (if no allergies)

Sesame or poppy seeds to sprinkle on top

Directions

Add all the dry ingredients to a large bowl. Stir to combine and break up any lumps.

Add the yoghurt and using the back of a spoon, push the yoghurt through the dry ingredients. It will seem a bit dry at this point. Finish mixing by squeezing the dough with your hands to completely move all the yoghurt through the dry ingredients to form a moist ball of dough. (If your coconut flour is extra course you may need to add an extra tablespoon of yoghurt).

The dough is now ready to be used in your recipe. It's best to cover your bowl to prevent the dough drying out while you roll out your portions of pastry. Place between 2 sheets of baking paper and use a rolling pin to roll out the dough.

When using for sausage rolls, I divide into 3 portions. Roll out to a thin rectangle, measuring 28cm x 15cm after trimmed. Spoon your sausage mixture 4cm in from the long side of the rolled pastry. Use the baking paper to lift the edge of the pastry and roll it over to enclose the filling. Turn the sausage roll so the seam is underneath. Cut into small sausage rolls or desired size (to make a neat clean cut, wipe your knife between each cut), also reroll the pastry trimmings. Place the sausage rolls onto a lined baking tray and brush with an egg wash or melted ghee and sprinkle with white or black sesame seeds. Bake at 170c (fan-forced) for 25 minutes.

When making pasties, divide dough into 10 portions (roughly 53g each) and roll into balls. Place one ball between 2 sheets of paper and flatten with your palm, then roll out into a 14 - 15cm round. Place your cooked filling on one half of the round leaving edges free to seal (use approx. 2 spoonfuls of filling). Use the baking paper to lift and assist as you fold the dough in half enclosing the filling. Press the edges together to seal and then roll the sealed edges in towards the filled section to create a neat edge. Use a skewer to poke 2 holes in the top of each pasty. Brush the tops with egg or melted ghee and sprinkle with poppy seeds. Bake at 170c (fan-forced) for 20 - 25 minutes.

Pie Crust

A mild flavoured almond meal piecrust that can be used for sweet or savoury pies. Pre-bake and fill with a dessert filling or with a savoury quiche filling.

Makes: 1 x 23cm   **Prep time:** 10 mins   **Cooking time:** 15 mins

---

Ingredients

SWEET CRUST

195g (1¾ cups) almond meal/flour (from blanched almonds)

1 Tbsp coconut flour

¼ tsp fine sea salt

2 Tbsp coconut oil, softened

1 large egg

1 Tbsp unprocessed honey

¾ tsp vanilla extract (organic)

SAVOURY CRUST

195g almond meal/flour

1 Tbsp coconut flour

¾ tsp Herbamare or ½ tsp sea salt

2 Tbsp coconut oil, soft

1 large egg

Directions

Preheat oven to 160c (fan-forced). Grease a 23cm pie dish with coconut oil.

Add the almond meal, coconut flour and salt (or Herbamare for savoury piecrust), and process for 8 seconds to combine and create a finer texture.

Add the coconut oil and egg (plus honey and vanilla for a sweet piecrust), and process for 10 seconds to bring the mixture together. If the savoury dough needs a little extra moisture, add 1 – 2 teaspoons of water while processing.

Use your hands to press the dough evenly into the pie dish and up the sides. Neaten or trim the edges. Prick the base of the pie in a few places with a fork or you can also cover the base with a circle of baking paper and place some baking weights on top to prevent the base rising. (Remove the weights for the last few minutes of baking).

Bake for 15 minutes or until lightly golden. If you find the base rises, press down gently with the back of a spoon before it cools and becomes firm. Allow the piecrust to cool completely before adding your pie filling. If you are baking a quiche add your ingredients into the pre-baked piecrust and place back into the oven.

Sweet Coconut Piecrust

(nut-free)

This is a perfect crisp and flaky piecrust that works well for an apple pie. The texture is very easy to roll. Double the recipe if you are covering the top of your pie or topping it with strips to make a crisscross pattern. The piecrust is pre-baked before filling.

Makes: 1 pie crust   **Prep time:** 15 mins   **Cooking time:** 18 mins

Ingredients

2 Tbsp golden flaxseed meal

3 Tbsp filtered water

215g (2¼ cups) desiccated coconut (organic)

42g (⅓ cup) arrowroot flour or tapioca

1 Tbsp unprocessed honey

¼ tsp fine sea salt

1 large egg

1 tsp vanilla extract (organic)

Directions

Preheat oven to 150c (fan-forced). Grease a deep 23cm pie dish with coconut oil.

Add the flaxseed and water to a small bowl, mix and set aside.

Add the coconut, arrowroot, honey and salt to a food processor. Process until the mixture has a fine texture, approximately 3 – 3½ minutes. Stop from time to time to scrape down the sides and base of the processor bowl.

Add the flaxseed mixture, egg and vanilla. Process for 30 seconds or until all the ingredients come together and have turned into a soft dough. Place the dough on a sheet of baking paper (if the dough is a little sticky, dust with a little arrowroot flour) and press the dough out to a circle with your hands. Place a further sheet of paper on top and use a rolling pin to roll out the dough. Make it larger than the pie dish, approximately 33cms in diameter.

Remove the top layer of paper and slip your hand under the bottom sheet and gently turn the dough over to place over the pie dish. Carefully lift the sides of the dough to allow it to slip down into the dish and then press the dough into the pie dish. Use a knife to trim the edges and if any splits occur it's soft enough to just press together to repair. Use a fork to prick the base in several places to prevent the piecrust rising off the bottom.

Pre-bake the piecrust for 18 - 20 minutes or until lightly golden, don't over cook. Cool the piecrust before adding your filling and then bake your pie as normal.

NOTE: Double the recipe if you plan to add a top to your pie or if you are making a crisscross pattern. For a pattern cut 8 strips of pastry with a pizza cutter (approx. 2.5cm wide). Place one strip at a time on top of the filled pie, (4 in total spaced evenly over the filled pie). Repeat, crossing over with the second layer of 4 strips. Press the ends of the strips neatly onto the rim of the piecrust. Bake for 25 minutes or until the strips have started to brown and are firm.

Pie and Tart Pastry Shells
(egg-free)

This recipe works really well for pastry shells, as it becomes lovely and firm once baked. Use a muffin tin to prebake your pastry and fill with leftover Bolognese or stew to make small pies. For sweet pastry shells, add a tablespoon of honey, they are excellent for mini lemon tarts. The ideas are endless for this pastry.

Makes: 14 muffin size shells **Prep time:** 15 mins **Cooking time:** 10 mins

Ingredients

220g (2 cups) almond meal (from blanched almonds)

95g (¾ cup) arrowroot flour or tapioca

28g (¼ cup) coconut flour

½ tsp baking soda (bicarb)

½ tsp fine sea salt

80ml macadamia oil or mild flavoured olive oil (plus extra for greasing tins)

80ml filtered water

Directions

Preheat oven to 170c (fan-forced). Grease 2 large muffin tins or tart tins with oil.

Add the almond meal, arrowroot, coconut flour, baking soda and salt to a food processor. Process for 6 - 8 seconds to mix the flours together. Add the oil and water and process for 20 seconds or until the mixture comes together into a very soft and pliable dough but not sticky. (Different brands of coconut flour can absorb more moisture than others, if the dough is too firm add 2 teaspoons of water, if too sticky add 1 teaspoon of coconut flour and process in). The softer the dough, the easier it is to mould into the muffin cups without it breaking or cracking.

Take half of the dough and roll between 2 sheets of baking paper to a thickness of 0.5cm. (You don't want the dough too thin). Use a large glass or jar with an opening of 9cm to cut out your circles of dough for a muffin tin or smaller for tarts. Lift a cut circle over the muffin or tart cup and gently tuck the sides in a little to shape it slightly like a cup and pop into the greased hole. Press the pastry into the base and sides. Use a fork to prick the base. Repeat with the remaining portion of dough.

Bake for 10 – 12 minutes or until crisp. Set aside for 5 minutes before adding the filling.

To make the Pies: Fill the baked pastry shells with Bolognese sauce or leftover thick stew (don't remove the shells from the tin). I like to use a topping of nut 'cheese' spread (if you tolerate dairy you can use crumbled feta cheese for a topping). Bake for 20 minutes or until heated through. Sit for 5 minutes before removing from the muffin tins.

To make Tarts: Add 1 tablespoon of honey to your pastry mixture when blending the ingredients. Remove the cooled baked pastry shells and fill them with lemon curd or filling of your choice.

SOMETHING A LITTLE SWEETER

Pancakes

These delicious Paleo pancakes are incredibly light and fluffy, you won't believe they are grain-free. Separating the eggs and adding a small amount of arrowroot flour help achieve the light and fluffy texture.

Makes: 12   Prep time: 10 mins   Cooking time: 20 mins

Ingredients

3 large eggs, separated (room temperature)

250ml almond or cashew milk (or milk of choice)

1 Tbsp 100% maple syrup or to taste

2 tsp vanilla extract (organic)

195g (1¾ cups) almond meal/flour (from blanched almonds)

3 Tbsp arrowroot flour or tapioca

½ tsp baking soda (bicarb)

Pinch fine sea salt

Ghee for cooking

Directions

Add the egg whites to a medium bowl and beat until stiff peaks form, then set aside.

Add the egg yolks, milk, maple syrup and vanilla to a large bowl and beat to combine.

Add the almond meal, arrowroot flour, baking soda and salt to the egg yolk and milk mixture and beat to blend all the ingredients together well.

Using a spatula, fold half the beaten egg whites into the batter and then fold in the remaining egg whites.

Heat a large non-stick frying pan on medium heat. Smear a coat of ghee over the pan.

Pour ¼ cup of the mixture into the pan for each pancake. Depending on the size of your pan, cook 2 or more at a time. Cook the pancakes for 3 - 4 minutes on the first side and use your spatula to left an edge to check it's cooked and firm before turning (the top will still be a little wet so turn carefully). Gently flip and cook the second side for approximately 2 minutes or until cooked through. Add extra ghee to the pan as needed.

Transfer the cooked pancakes to a plate and keep warm. Repeat with the remaining batter.

Serve with maple syrup, coconut yoghurt or whipped cashew cream and berries.

Note: This recipe can also be used to make pikelets (use 2 tablespoons of batter per pikelet).

Coconut Flour Waffles (nut-free)

Light and fluffy nut-free waffles your family will love. My favourite way to serve them is with maple syrup, coconut yoghurt, berries and a sprinkle of cinnamon.

Makes: 3 lge   **Prep time:** 05 mins   **Cooking time:** 15 mins

Ingredients

35g (⅓ cup) coconut flour, sifted

3 Tbsp arrowroot flour or tapioca

1 tsp baking powder (gluten free)

¼ tsp fine sea salt

4 large eggs

125ml (½ cup) canned coconut milk (a thick brand like Ayam)

80g (⅓ cup) ghee or grass-fed butter, melted

2 Tbsp (40ml) mild flavoured olive oil

1 Tbsp 100% maple syrup

1 tsp vanilla extract (organic)

Directions

Preheat your waffle maker. The temperature will depend on the brand of waffle maker you have, I find mine needs to be on high and cook a little longer when using coconut flour. Follow your manufactures instructions for use and if you need to grease your machine, use a pastry brush to lightly coat with oil or ghee.

Add the coconut flour, arrowroot, baking powder and salt to a large bowl. Stir to mix the flours together.

Add the eggs, coconut milk, melted ghee/butter, olive oil, maple syrup and vanilla. Use a handheld electric beater and beat on low to mix the ingredients together, then increase to medium speed to produce a smooth thick batter with no lumps.

Spoon the mixture into the bottom grid of the waffle maker; you want just enough to reach the peak area. Use the back of a spoon or a spatula to spread the batter out evenly. The batter thins out and spreads easier as it hits the hot waffle plate. Close and seal, then rotate the machine by the handle to make sure the batter is evenly distributed and cooked. Rotate the machine back to check if the waffle is sufficiently done. Cook for approximately 4 - 5 minutes or until golden brown. Repeat with the remaining batter.

Serve with your favourite toppings.

Cooled waffles can be reheated individually by returning them to the hot waffle maker and reheat for 2 minutes on low-medium heat, be careful not to burn them or you can pop them into a toaster.

Chocolate Donuts (nut-free)

These moist nut-free chocolate donuts are perfect for children to take to school to celebrate a birthday. No one will even know they are made from healthy coconut flour.

Makes: 10 **Prep time:** 15 mins **Cooking time:** 20 mins

Ingredients

35g (⅓ cup) coconut flour
28g (⅓ cup) cacao powder
3 Tbsp arrowroot flour or tapioca
½ tsp baking soda (bicarb)
¼ tsp fine sea salt
4 large eggs
80ml (⅓ cup) 100% maple syrup, or to taste
60ml (¼ cup) canned coconut milk (a thick brand like Ayam)
2 tsp vanilla extract (organic)
1 tsp apple cider vinegar
80g (⅓ cup) coconut oil, melted

CHOCOLATE TOPPING
70g organic dark chocolate, broken into pieces (I use 80% chocolate)
1 Tbsp coconut oil
1 tsp 100% maple syrup
¾ tsp vanilla extract (organic)
Decorative toppings (I've used Hoppers natural sprinkles, nuts, beetroot powder, fresh flowers and coconut).

Directions

Preheat oven to 175c (fan-forced). Use silicon donut molds (I've used a 7.5cm/3in diameter mold) or grease a donut tin well and place the molds on a large tray.

Add the coconut flour, cacao powder, arrowroot, baking soda and salt to a food processor. Process for 10 – 15 seconds to combine well and create a fine texture.

Add the eggs, maple syrup, coconut milk, vanilla, vinegar and coconut oil. Process for 15 – 18 seconds, you will have a thin batter but it will thicken quite quickly.

Add the batter to a jug and pour or spoon the batter around the well of each donut mold, fill each ¾ full.

Bake for 20 minutes or until the batter is set on top, don't over cook. Allow the donuts to cool in the mold for 5 – 10 minutes before carefully popping the donuts out. Turn them over and finish cooling on a wire rack (you will decorate the rounded bottoms).

To make the chocolate topping: Melt the chocolate and coconut oil together while continually whisking. Remove from heat and whisk in the maple syrup and vanilla.

Once the chocolate topping cools to a thick pouring consistency, spoon or drizzle the chocolate around the tops of the donuts, then sprinkle with your decorative toppings. Let the donuts sit or pop in the fridge for a few minutes to allow the chocolate to set.

Cinnamon Scrolls

You will find pecans, cinnamon and honey rolled up in these yummy soft centered and chewy on the outside scrolls. Once the scrolls are drizzled with my vanilla coconut glaze you won't be able to resist them.

Makes: 8   **Prep time:** 20 mins   **Cooking time:** 15 mins

Ingredients

250g (2¼ cups) almond meal/flour (from blanched almonds)

33g (¼ cup) arrowroot flour or tapioca

1½ Tbsp golden flaxseed meal

2 tsp baking powder (gluten free)

¼ tsp fine sea salt

2 large eggs

1 Tbsp honey

1 tsp vanilla extract (organic)

1 Tbsp coconut oil, melted

FILLING:

¼ cup honey

1 Tbsp cinnamon

½ cup finely chopped pecans

VANILLA GLAZE:

60ml (¼ cup) coconut milk

60g (¼ cup) coconut oil

2 tsp honey

1 tsp vanilla extract (organic)

1 tsp arrowroot flour

Directions

Preheat oven to 160c (fan-forced). Line a baking tray with baking paper.

Add the almond meal, arrowroot, golden flaxseed, baking powder and salt to a large bowl. Mix well to combine and remove any lumps.

Add the eggs, honey and vanilla to a small bowl and whisk to combine. Add the coconut oil while still whisking. Pour the wet mixture into the bowl of dry ingredients and mix well, then finish mixing with your hands to produce a smooth dough.

Place the dough on a sheet of baking paper and shape into a rectangle. Place a second sheet of paper on top and roll out using a rolling pin to measure a 30 x 28cm rectangle.

Remove the top sheet of paper and add the filling. Drizzle the honey over the dough, spread evenly then sprinkle with cinnamon and the pecans.

Roll the dough from the long side using the paper underneath to help you carefully roll the dough as tight as possible. Press down on the paper as you roll but don't allow it to get caught up in the dough. Roll until you have a nice even log and if any splits occur just press and smooth through the paper to mend.

Trim off 1cm from each end of the roll and discard. Use a sharp knife to cut the roll into 8 – 10 even pieces (I cut mine in 3cm slices). Place each piece with flat side down on the prepared tray (clean the knife between cuts). Leave a little space between each piece.

Bake for 15 minutes until the scrolls are golden and the centres are still soft but not doughy. Allow to cool on the tray for 10 minutes and serve warm or cold drizzled with the glaze.

To make the glaze: Add all the glaze ingredients to a small saucepan. Continually whisk while heating over low heat until the milk and oil has emulsified and the glaze has slightly thickened. Don't allow to boil. Set aside to cool but not set.

Banana and Choc Chip Muffins (nut-free)

Your family will love these delicious nut-free, light and moist banana choc chip muffins. This is a no-fuss recipe that can be whipped up in minutes, making them perfect for lunchboxes.

Makes: 12   **Prep time:** 10 mins   **Cooking time:** 25 mins

Ingredients

2 large eggs

3 large ripe bananas

125g (½ cup) tahini, hulled or sunflower seed butter

80g (⅓ cup) ghee or coconut oil

2 Tbsp 100% maple syrup

2 tsp vanilla extract (organic)

52g (½ cup) coconut flour

1 Tbsp cinnamon

2 tsp baking powder (gluten free)

¼ tsp fine sea salt

½ cup organic 70% dark chocolate chips (or chopped chocolate)

Directions

Preheat oven to 170c (fan-forced). Line a large muffin tin with paper liners or use a good quality silicon muffin tray.

Add the eggs, banana, tahini (or sunflower butter), ghee, maple syrup and vanilla to a food processor. Process for 20 seconds to combine and create a smooth texture with no banana bits. Scape down sides of the bowl.

Add the coconut flour, cinnamon, baking powder and salt. Process for approximately 20 seconds to combine all the ingredients together well. Remove the blade and stir through the chocolate chips by hand.

Spoon the mixture evenly between the muffin holes, approximately ¾ cup for each (for young children you may want to use smaller muffin cups and adjust the cooking time). Use the back of a teaspoon to smooth the top.

Bake for 25 - 30 minutes or until cooked through, turn once during cooking for an even colour.

Allow to cool in the tin for 10 minutes, then remove and finish cooling on a wire rack.

Store in an airtight container in the fridge for up to 5 days, also suitable to freeze.

Blueberry and Coconut Flour Muffins (nut-free option)

Adding almond extract to these muffins really complements the blueberries and gives a delicious flavour. Extra eggs are required for coconut flour recipes, as they are needed to bind the ingredients together. You are going to love these light, soft muffins. See notes below for nut-free option.

Makes: 10   **Prep time:** 15 mins   **Cooking time:** 25 mins

Ingredients

125g (½ cup) ghee or coconut oil

80g (⅓ cup) unprocessed honey

52g (½ cup) coconut flour, sifted

65g (½ cup) arrowroot flour or tapioca

2 tsp baking powder (gluten free)

¼ tsp fine sea salt

5 large eggs, room temperature

1 tsp vanilla extract (organic)

1 tsp almond extract (organic)

125g (1 cup) blueberries or frozen blueberries (organic)

Almond flakes or shredded coconut to sprinkle on top

Directions

Preheat oven to 180c (fan-forced). Place paper liners into a large muffin tin or use a silicon muffin tray.

Add the ghee and honey to a small saucepan and melt but don't allow it to get too hot. Set aside.

Add the coconut flour, arrowroot, baking powder and salt to a large bowl. Mix well to combine.

Add the eggs, vanilla and almond extract to the dry ingredients, then pour in the cooled but melted ghee and honey. Beat using a hand-held electric beater to produce a smooth batter.

Fold the blueberries gently into the batter using a spatula (you can add extra blueberries if you prefer). If you are using frozen berries don't allow them to thaw or you will get purple juice through the batter.

Spoon the batter into the prepared muffin tin, filling each ¾ full. Use the back of a spoon to smooth the tops. Add a few almond flakes or some coconut to the top of each muffin and press lightly down.

Bake for 25 – 30 minutes until firm and golden. Let the muffins cool in the tin for 10 minutes then transfer them to a wire rack to finish cooling.

Store in an airtight container in the fridge. Suitable to freeze.

For nut-free: Omit almond extract and increase the vanilla to 2 teaspoons and use coconut to sprinkle on top.

Fruity Nut Scones

This scone variation will impress any visitors with their combination of different flavours and textures.

Makes: 12   Prep time: 15 mins   Cooking time: 15 mins

Ingredients

220g (2 cups) almond meal/flour (from blanched almonds)

65g (½ cup) arrowroot flour or tapioca

⅓ cup pistachios, roughly chopped

40g (¼ cup) sesame seeds

40g (¼ cup) sunflower seeds

¾ tsp baking soda (bicarb)

½ tsp fine sea salt

⅓ cup organic dried blueberries or freeze dried (or fruit of choice)

5 Medjool dates, pitted and chopped

2 Tbsp 100% maple syrup

1 Tbsp mild olive oil or macadamia oil

1 large egg

Directions

Preheat oven to 160c (fan-forced). Line a baking tray with baking paper.

Add the almond meal, arrowroot, pistachios, sesame seeds, sunflower seeds, baking soda and salt to a large bowl. Stir to mix well, then add the blueberries and dates, and stir to evenly distribute them through the dry ingredients.

Add the maple syrup, olive oil and egg to a small bowl and whisk to combine.

Pour the wet ingredients into the dry and mix well, then use your hands to finish combining the mixture to create a moist dough.

Place the dough on a sheet of baking paper and shape into a rectangle, approximately 16 x 14cms with a thickness of 2.5cm. Dust a large knife in arrowroot to prevent sticking and cut the dough into 4 x 3 rows, making 12 scones.

Place the scones onto the prepared tray and bake for 15 minutes or until just lightly golden.

Serve warm with grass-fed butter or ghee, or just as they are.

Ginger Loaf

This delightful ginger loaf is perfect for afternoon tea with guests or just when a healthy snack is needed. It's a favourite in our home with its warm sweet flavours and moist texture.

Makes: 1 loaf   **Prep time:** 20 mins   **Cooking time:** 40 mins

---

Ingredients

10 large Medjool dates, pitted and soaked in boiling water

195g (1¾ cups) almond meal (from blanched almonds)

3 Tbsp golden flaxseed meal

1 Tbsp ground ginger

2 tsp cinnamon

1 tsp ground coriander

1 tsp baking soda (bicarb)

⅓ tsp fine sea salt

2 large eggs

1 Tbsp 100% maple syrup

2 tsp apple cider vinegar

2 tsp vanilla extract (organic)

80g (⅓ cup) coconut oil, melted

Directions

Preheat oven to 160c (fan-forced). Line a 21 x 10cm loaf tin with baking paper.

Soak the dates in boiling water for 10 - 15 minutes. Drain and add to a food processor and blend for a few seconds to create a thick paste. Scrap down the sides of the bowl.

Add the remaining ingredients in order to the food processor and blend to combine well (approximately 12 – 15 seconds).

Scoop the mixture into the prepared tin and use a spatula to smooth the top.

Bake for 40 minutes or until firm to the touch and starting to come away from the sides of the tin.

Allow to cool in the tin for 15 minutes before removing. Place on a wire rack to completely cool before slicing. Store in an airtight container or slice and freeze.

Serve plain or spread with grass-fed butter or ghee.

Chocolate Zucchini Bread

(nut-free)

This moist chocolaty nut-free bread is a great way to hide some vegetable and fruit into your families snack. This is a great treat to pack in school lunch-boxes. Zucchini contains flavonoids, which fight free radicals in the body and are an excellent source of potassium and vitamin C.

Makes: 1 loaf **Prep time:** 20 mins **Cooking time:** 60 mins

Ingredients

3 large eggs
1 large ripe banana, broken in half
125ml (½ cup) 100% maple syrup or honey
80ml (⅓ cup) coconut cream or yoghurt
1 Tbsp vanilla extract (organic)
1 tsp apple cider vinegar
75g (⅔ cup) golden flaxseed meal
35g (⅓ cup) coconut flour

33g (¼ cup) arrowroot flour or tapioca
40g (½ cup) raw cacao powder
1 Tbsp cinnamon
1 tsp baking soda (bicarb)
½ tsp fine sea salt
1 cup grated zucchini, firmly packed with liquid squeezed out

Directions

Preheat oven to 160c (fan-forced). Line a 21 x 10cm loaf tin with baking paper.

Add the eggs, banana, maple syrup, coconut cream, vanilla and apple cider vinegar to a food processor. Blend for 10 seconds, then scrape down the sides.

Add the flaxseed, coconut flour, arrowroot, cacao, cinnamon, baking soda and salt. Blend for 15 seconds to combine well and scrape down the sides.

Use a few sheets of paper towel or a tea towel to squeeze the liquid out of the grated zucchini. Add the zucchini and blend for a further 12 - 15 seconds (there shouldn't be any zucchini shreds visible).

Scoop the mixture into the prepared tin and use a spatula to smooth the top.

Bake for 60 - 65 minutes or until a skewer inserted comes out clean. Allow to cool in the tin for 15 minutes. Remove by lifting out by the baking paper and finish cooling on a wire rack.

To serve: use a small sieve and push a little cacao powder through to decorate the top. Delicious served with dollops of vanilla coconut yoghurt.

Store in an airtight container in the fridge for up to 7 days. Serve at room temperature. Suitable to freeze (it's best to slice first).

Spiced Pumpkin Bread

This easy, sweetly spiced pumpkin bread recipe is absolutely delicious. It's high in protein and fibre, making it perfect for a healthy snack.

Makes: 1 loaf   **Prep time:** 10 mins   **Cooking time:** 60 mins

---

Ingredients

220g (2 cups) almond meal/flour (from blanched almonds)

30g (¼ cup) golden flaxseed meal

1 Tbsp cinnamon

1 tsp ground ginger

1 tsp allspice

¾ tsp baking soda (bicarb)

¼ tsp fine sea salt

235g (1 cup) mashed pumpkin, cook ahead and cool

3 Tbsp unprocessed honey

4 large eggs

Directions

Preheat oven to 160c (fan-forced). Line a 21 x 10cm loaf tin with baking paper.

Add the almond meal, flaxseed, cinnamon, ginger, allspice, baking soda and salt to a food processor. Process for 10 seconds to mix the ingredients.

Add the mashed pumpkin, honey and eggs. Process for 12 – 15 seconds to combine well.

Spoon the batter into the prepared tin and smooth over the top.

Bake for 60 minutes or until a skewer inserted comes out clean. Allow to cool in the tin for 15 minutes then transfer to a wire rack to finish cooling.

Store in an airtight container in the fridge for up to 7 days, also suitable to freeze.

Apricot and Carrot Loaf

A deliciously moist fruit and vegetable loaf that's perfect for a healthy breakfast or afternoon tea. Use organic apricots to avoid the preservative, sulphur dioxide.

Makes: 1 loaf   **Prep time:** 15 mins   **Cooking time:** 45 mins

Ingredients

1 cup grated carrot

¾ cup diced organic dried apricots

165g (1½ cups) almond meal/flour (from blanched almonds)

35g (⅓ cup) coconut flour

33g (¼ cup) arrowroot or tapioca flour

1 Tbsp cinnamon, plus extra to sprinkle on top to serve

½ tsp nutmeg

¾ tsp baking soda (bicarb)

¼ tsp fine sea salt

80g (⅓ cup) coconut oil, melted

80g (⅓ cup) unprocessed honey

4 large eggs

1 Tbsp vanilla extract (organic)

2 tsp apple cider vinegar

Directions

Preheat oven to 170c (fan-forced). Line a 21 × 10cm loaf tin with baking paper.

Grate the carrot and dice apricots and set aside.

Add the almond meal, coconut flour, arrowroot, cinnamon, nutmeg, baking soda and salt to a food processor. Process for 15 seconds to combine and produce a finer texture.

Add the carrot, coconut oil, honey, eggs, vanilla and vinegar. Process for 10 seconds then scrape down sides of the bowl.

Add the apricot pieces evenly around the bowl and pulse a couple of times to stir through the mixture without breaking them up.

Scoop the mixture into the prepared tin and smooth the top. Bake for 45 – 50 minutes until the loaf is starting to come away from the sides.

Allow to cool in the tin for 15 minutes before lifting out by the baking paper, finish cooling on a wire rack. Once completely cooled, sprinkle the top with extra cinnamon and slice.

Store in a sealed container in the fridge, suitable to freeze (1 slice before freezing).

Chocolate Chip Shortbread
(nut & egg-free)

This is such an easy nut and egg free recipe. It has a delicious buttery flavour; you can swap the ghee for coconut oil (but you get a stronger coconut flavour). These chocolate chip shortbread wedges are a delicious healthy afternoon tea treat and perfect for school lunchboxes.

Serves: 8   **Prep time:** 15 mins   **Cooking time:** 15 mins

Ingredients

52g (½ cup) coconut flour

65g (½ cup) arrowroot flour

¼ tsp fine sea salt

80g (⅓ cup) ghee or grass-fed butter (coconut oil can also be used)

3 Tbsp 100% maple syrup

½ tsp vanilla extract

¼ cup 70% organic dark chocolate chips

Directions

Preheat oven to 170c (fan-forced).

Add the coconut flour, arrowroot and salt to a food processor and process for 10 – 15 seconds to combine and create a finer texture (if your coconut flour is very coarse, process a little longer).

Add the ghee, maple syrup and vanilla then process until the mixture comes together (approx. 15 seconds). Scape down sides of the bowl and remove the blade.

Add the chocolate chips and push them through the mixture with the back of a spoon.

Scrape the mixture onto a sheet of baking paper and bring together with your hands. Use your fingers to push out the mixture to a 21cm circle, smooth the surface with your hands and make sure the edges are the same thickness as the centre.

Slide the paper with the dough onto a baking tray. Use a pizza cutter or large knife to cut the circle into quarters and then into eighths.

Bake for 15 minutes or until golden (if your oven doesn't brown evenly, turn the tray at the halfway point). Allow to completely cool on the tray and then once cool, slice through the cut lines to make sure you get a clean edge to your shortbread wedges.

Store in a glass airtight container.

ACKNOWLEDGEMENTS

A BIG THANK YOU:

To you my readers and supporters who have continued to encourage me to keep on creating new healthy recipes. You have expressed that bread was the hardest to give up, even though you knew it was detrimental to your health. You gave me the inspiration to create this book. Please enjoy the many recipes in this book as they were created with you in mind.

To my family: I'm so fortunate to have a husband and family that supports me in my endeavours. My darling hubby Bryan has continued to clean up after me and wash the many piles of dishes that were created during recipe experimenting (but he does like the food reward at the end), you are the best. To my daughter-in-law Clare, who has had her own digestive issues, thank you for helping me to create healing food that assisted to improve your gut health. Your feed back and positive results gave me the inspiration and reason to help those with similar problems. To my grandchildren, for being the most honest taste testers and critics.

To Jacque, for patiently proof reading my writing and picking up all my spelling and grammar errors. You gave up your time to help make this book just right.

Index

CPSIA information can be obtained
at www.ICGtesting.com
Printed in the USA
BVHW091743080321
602014BV00003B/163